Beer on the

The Craft Breweries of Alaska

Volume Two:
Anchorage, Fairbanks, & Everything In Between

By Bill Howell
Photos by Elaine Howell

Foreword by Gabe Fletcher, Anchorage Brewing Company

Finally! Someone has written a book about craft brewing in Alaska. Brewing in Alaska has a longer history than most people realize. Back in the day it took an adventurous spirit and a determination that would bring most to their knees. That determination still lives on in the few souls that have decide to start a brewery in Alaska.

In the early 90s when craft beer really started to enter the Alaska market, people didn't know how to react to it. Some loved it, and some just kept to their yellow fizzy beer. The brewers stuck to their guns, pushing the envelope of brewing and creating new flavors that their customers just couldn't resist. Eventually, it really caught on and now there's a huge culture of what we call "beer geeks" out there that just can't seem to get enough of this creative elixir!

People love coming to the source to talk with these brewers and see how they craft their beer, learn about what's coming out next, and find out where they can get it. Even the way people drink beer up here has changed. It can be like a ritual for some... Pulling the beer out of the cooler like it is the Holy Grail for all to see. Choosing just the right vessel that will complement the style of beer. Carefully pouring it into the glass, just fast enough to create the perfect head, but stopping at the bottle's end to leave the yeast behind. Taking a sniff followed by a taste... the conversation begins. After enjoying every last drop, maybe they follow up with a review on their Beer Up Here app on their iPhone. All of this could be happening while catching a 50 pound King Salmon on a fly rod! Talk about multitasking...

If there is anyone out there that could write a book about Alaska Breweries, it's Bill Howell. He is a local beer writer and one of the most passionate "beer geeks" of all things beer up here. Bill is also a contributor to Northwest Brewing News and has won the coveted and very difficult Beer Drinker of the Year award in Denver.

Alaska breweries are thriving more than ever right now and it seems like there is a new one opening every month. I wouldn't be surprised if we doubled the number of breweries in ten years. I guess Bill will have to start working on his sequel to this book!

Here's to the Beer on the Last Frontier! May it always thrive and continue to give us delicious liquid gold!

Cheers,

Gabe Fletcher

Founder/Brewer

Anchorage Brewing Company

Table of Contents

Introduction

As anyone who has ever been here can tell you, Alaska is a special place. Sometimes it's special in a good way, sometimes it's special in a bad way, but it's never ordinary. Here in The Great Land, we live a lot closer to the edge than most people do Outside (what Alaskans call the rest of the world). Those folks can tell themselves that Nature has been tamed by Man; we Alaskans know better.

Looking out the authors' living room window on 6/20/2011

It takes a certain kind of person to choose to live in a place as remote and rugged as Alaska. Some people are born to it, but choose to leave as soon as they can. Often they return after a year or two, finding nowhere else in the world holds the allure of the Far North.

Others come up for a visit or a vacation or a job and never leave. Be Warned: If Alaska grabs hold of you, no other place in the whole wide world will ever seem like home again.

Alaska is unique in its climate, its wildlife and the people who live here. Is it any surprise that our beers are unique as well? Beers, wines, meads, distilled spirits: they are all made commercially here in Alaska. And not just made, but made well. Alaska's alcoholic beverages are the frequent winners of awards in national and even international competitions. There are 24 commercial breweries in Alaska, two wineries, a meadery, and four distilleries. Not bad for a state with under 800,000 total residents.

This book is an exploration and guide to the craft breweries making exceptional beers for Alaskans to drink. This volume covers Anchorage, Fairbanks, and all points in between. Volume I, published in 2012, covered the Kenai Peninsula and Kodiak Island. Volume III will cover Southeast Alaska. It is not intended to be a stand-alone guide to the parts of Alaska it covers. Rather, it should be viewed as a supplement, one which will point the visitor who is particularly interested in experiencing craft beer in Alaska in the right direction.

Anchorage

Unless they are visiting Alaska solely via a cruise through the Inside Passage, it's the rare visitor to the state who does not pass through Anchorage. With over 40% of the entire state's population, Anchorage dominates Alaska in many ways. Even those Alaskans who do not live within its confines often find themselves drawn there, either for business, shopping, travel, or other reasons.

Huge as it may be by Alaskan standards, Anchorage remains a small city located in the midst of the wilderness. There is a great deal of wildlife within its boundaries; moose sighting are frequent, and the possibility of a bear encounter is always there, so visitors are well advised to be on their toes and to keep a camera handy.

For the beer lover, Anchorage (and the Mat-Su Valley bedroom communities that support it) presents the greatest concentration of breweries and brewpubs in the state. With six breweries/brewpubs currently operating within city limits and two more less than an hour's drive to the north, the beer traveler would do well to allow themselves a couple of days at the very least to experience all that Anchorage has to offer them.

Anchorage is also home to several beer festivals scattered throughout the year; depending on when you visit, one of these might make a good option. Most of them take place outside the busy Memorial Day to Labor Day tourist season; we Alaskans like to keep our best beers to ourselves. But if you are brave enough to visit The Great Land during the winter, we'll happily share some of the finest beers in the world with you.

The Matanuska-Susitna Valley

Located to the northeast of Anchorage, the Matanuska-Susitna Valley is both a bedroom community for the city of Anchorage and one of the prime farming areas of Alaska. Hemmed in by water and mountains, real estate in the Anchorage bowl is at a premium, so most of the recent population growth has taken place in this area, known to locals as the Mat-Su or even just The Valley.

The Valley is currently home to the Arkose Brewery and the Last Frontier Brewing Company, located in Palmer and Wasilla, respectively. Palmer is also home to the Alaska Sate Fair, held in the last two weeks of August every year, and the brewery is located very near to the fairgrounds, so if you visit during that timeframe, plan accordingly. Wasilla rose to national prominence as the hometown of former Alaska governor and 2008 candidate for Vice President, Sarah Palin. The main highway running north from Anchorage to Denali National Park and Fairbanks, along with the Alaska Railroad, passes right through downtown Wasilla and right past The Last Frontier Brewing Company, a brewpub.

Denali National Park and the Parks Highway

The Parks Highway continues north from Wasilla and The Valley, towards Denali National Park, Healy, and eventually Fairbanks. By the way, the highway's name has nothing to do with the National Park. Its full name is actually the George A. Parks Highway; he was the governor of the Territory of Alaska from 1925 to 1933.

About one hundred miles north of Anchorage, a spur road diverges from the Parks Highway to the funky mountain town of Talkeetna. Allegedly the inspiration for the fictional town of Ciciley, Alaska in the TV series **Northern Exposure**, Talkeetna is a bustling tourist destination in the summer and almost deserted during the off-season. It is home to the Denali Brewing Company, which has a large production brewery (and taproom) at Mile 2 of the spur road, and a smaller brewery and beer garden in downtown Talkeetna, co-located with the Twister Creek Restaurant.

Another 140 miles past Talkeetna on the Parks Highway brings you to the entrance to Denali National Park, and the strip of tourist-focused businesses in Nenana Canyon, often referred to by locals derisively as "Glitter Gulch". Another twelve miles north is the small community of Healy, home to the 49th State Brewing Company, which is only open during the warmer months, from April through October. From Healy, it is another 113 miles to Fairbanks.

Fairbanks

At the end of the Parks Highway, you will reach the second largest city in Alaska, Fairbanks. Nicknamed the Golden City, Fairbanks was established in 1903 in response to a mammoth gold strike in the region. Eventually the Alaska Railroad was constructed -- running from Seward on the Kenai Peninsula, north through Anchorage and then on to Fairbanks -- primarily to allow the transportation of heavy mining equipment to the area, which supported extensive gold dredge activity through the middle of the last century. Just as the gold mining activity began to wane, the opening of the Prudhoe Bay Oilfields on the North Slope gave Fairbanks new economic purpose as their major supply center.

From a beer-drinker's perspective, Fairbanks has long lagged behind the rest of the state. While the Silver

Gulch Brewing and Bottling Company (technically located in the tiny town of Fox, rather than Fairbanks itself) has been quite successful since it opened in 1997, for fifteen years it remained the <u>only</u> brewery in the vicinity of Alaska's second-largest city. It was not until the opening of HooDoo Brewing Company on October 31st, 2012, that Fairbanks gained a brewery within city limits. To date there is still no brewpub in the Fairbanks area.

Map

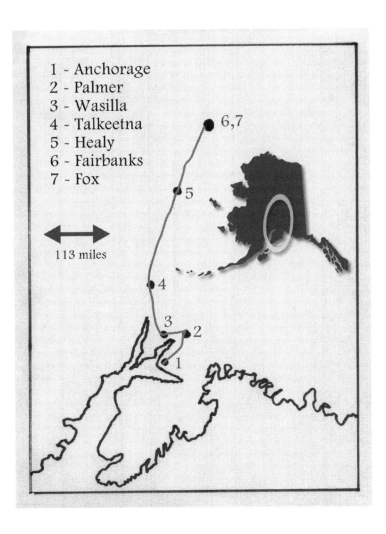

1 ~ Anchorage
2 ~ Palmer
3 ~ Wasilla
4 ~ Talkeetna
5 ~ Healy
6 ~ Fairbanks
7 ~ Fox

113 miles

Anchorage Breweries

Anchorage Brewing Company

Location:

717 W 3rd Ave

Anchorage, AK 99501

Phone: 907-360-5104

Email: anchoragebrewing@gmail.com

Website: www.anchoragebrewingcompany.com

Hours of Operation:

The brewery is not open to the public.

Driving Directions: The brewery is located in the basement beneath the Snow Goose Restaurant/Sleeping Lady Brewery. See their section for directions.

Overview

As far as the wider beer world is concerned, Gabe Fletcher is probably the best known brewmaster in Alaska. After a long and famously successful stint as the brewmaster for **Midnight Sun Brewing Company**, he decided to establish his own brewery in 2010. The **Anchorage Brewing Company**'s motto is "Where brewing is an art and Brettanomyces is king," so that gives you an idea of the sort of beers he's looking to make now.

When he decided to strike out on his own, Fletcher made two unusual (and, in hindsight, very smart) choices. First, rather than focus on the local beer market in Anchorage or even Alaska, he negotiated with Shelton Brothers to purchase and distribute the lion's share of his production across the country and even internationally. Fletcher's reputation in the beer world after his stint at Midnight Sun was such that they were happy to agree, even before he'd brewed his first batch. Second, rather than purchase his own brewhouse, Fletcher rented time on the existing brewhouse at the Sleeping Lady Brewing Company, as well as space in their basement to locate his fermenters, barrels, and bottling line. To be clear, this was not contract brewing, as Fletcher did all the brewing himself; he simply bought time on their equipment.

These two decision allowed Fletcher to focus his start-up capital on what would make his beers unique: huge wooden foudres for his primary fermentation, a forest of used wine and spirits barrels for secondary fermentation, and a state-of-art Italian bottling line to fill his 750ml corked and caged bottles. His amazing success over the last three years is testimony to the farsightedness of these two decisions.

Gabe Fletcher, the man behind Anchorage Brewing Company

Brewery Characteristics

As mentioned above, Anchorage Brewing Company rents time on the Sleeping Lady Brewing Company's brewhouse to produce their beers, so please see the entry on that brewery for details on the brewhouse itself. What makes Anchorage Brewing so unique is what happens after the beer leaves the brew kettle and gravity drains down one floor to the "Brett Cave".

Oak foudres and barrels waiting to be filled

First and foremost, every beer that Anchorage produces is fermented entirely in wood, with primary fermentation taking place in the foudres and secondary fermentation (if there is any) taking place in barrels, before being bottle conditioned before release. Second, every beer is dosed with Brettanomyces, reflecting Fletcher's fascination with that particular yeast strain.

Fletcher's interests extend beyond just Brettanomyces, however. He has constructed a coolship and begun experimenting with spontaneously fermented beers. He has produced sour ales, using both Pedioccocus and Lactobacillus bacteria. He has partnered with the Danish gypsy brewer Mikeller to produce several beers

Given that he is working with such temperamental elements, the release schedule for particular Anchorage Brewing Company beers can be quite fluid, at best. When asked about the release date for a particular brew, the answer Fletcher gives most often is, "When it's ready."

State of the art bottling line from Italy

Besides his primary focus on releasing his beers in bottles, Fletcher also produces the occasional one-off draft release, typically for distribution in the local area or as collaboration with another brewery.

The Brewer Speaks

Gabe Fletcher in his own words:

How did you become a commercial brewer?

I never set out to be a brewer, it just sort of fell in my lap. When I turned 21 I found myself going to the liquor store and always walking out with something new. I was fascinated with all of the different beers to choose from, and back then, it really wasn't much. I walked into this brew your own wine place one day and asked if they needed any help, and they did. I worked there for a bit just helping out anywhere I could. I received a call one day from Midnight Sun Brewing asking if I would like to come work for them. A person I used to work with at the wine place, started working there and recommended me to the brewery. I went in for an interview and that day I was put on the bottling line. Within a year and a half I learned the basics of brewing, an opening for head brewer opened up and I took it, promising the owners that I could do the job. It was daunting at first, but I eventually got in my groove and really started pushing the envelope of brewing, always trying new techniques and looking at brewing from a different angle. I put in almost 13 years there and finally decided it was time to move on and create my own brewery and start making beer on my own terms. That is where Anchorage Brewing Company was born. Now I focus on the things I love about brewing, Barrels and Brettanomyces. No more production brewing, I wanted to slow things down and make people wait for my beer instead of working to meet the schedule of the masses.

What do you see as the biggest challenges facing a craft brewer in Alaska?

The cost of shipping is always an issue, especially if you are shipping the grain and glass up to Alaska and then shipping the full bottles back down to distribute in the lower 48 or even Europe. Other than that, I don't see a lot of differences. There's always the snow factor, but that's just part of living in Alaska. We have amazing brewing water, and it's cold! There are many breweries in the lower 48 that need to filter the hell out of there water and then add all new minerals just to balance things out. There are also many that need cold liquor tanks because there water out of the tap isn't cold enough for certain parts of the brewing process. Though I think here in Anchorage we have it a little easier than say the breweries in Kodiak Island and Haines, but I can't speak for them.

What characteristics do you think define Alaskan craft beer, as opposed to craft beer brewed elsewhere?

I don't feel that there are any real characteristics that define Alaskan craft beer.

Where do you think Alaskan craft brewing in general and your brewery/brewpub in particular will be in eight to ten years?

I think Alaska State law will require all breweries to make all beers with Brettanomyces by the year 2015. I hope to have a new facility and a tasting room but after that I don't want to grow any more.

The Beers

Whiteout Wit: Pour a lovely light gold in color, absolutely crystal clear, and with a massive white head. This beer is perfect in an over-sized tulip glass (AKA a *Duvel*-style one), to give room for this huge head. Most wits are slightly cloudy, due to the wheat in the mash, but not this one. The aroma is very enticing: Spiciness, both from the yeast used and the actual addition of spices (coriander and peppercorns), and lemon-citrus notes, both from the use of lemon peel and Sorachi Ace hops. The beer is beautifully carbonated and wonderfully light on the palate. The flavor notes from the lemon and the spices blend beautifully with the woody notes from aging in French Oak Chardonnay barrels and the touch of tart funkiness from the secondary fermentation with Brettanomyces. The Brett notes are extremely well-balanced and totally integrated into the overall flavor profile, really becoming apparent only on the long finish. Made with Sorachi hops and spiced with fresh lemon peel, Indian coriander, and black peppercorns. Aged in French oak Chardonnay barrels. 6% ABV & 20 IBUs.

Bitter Monk Double IPA: Pours a clear, bright gold, with a massive white head of pin-point carbonation;

very beautiful in the glass. The aroma has lots of bright, Citra hop notes, likely from its dry-hopping, with the slightest whiff of Brettanomyces funk. On the palate the beer certainly lives up to its name, with the 100 IBUs being immediately apparent. As the hop shock to my taste buds began to subside, I could pick up the Brett, then a little woodiness from the oak aging, all falling away gradually to a nice, funky finish. This beer has a myriad of very strong flavors, all of which are dominated by its shattering bitterness. Aged in French oak Chardonnay barrels. 9% ABV & 100 IBUs.

Love Buzz Saison: Pours a deep, slightly cloudy gold, with a big, rocky white head. Citra hop aroma is present in the nose, which is not surprising since this beer is also dry-hopped with that variety. There are also the earthy, spicy notes that are typical of Belgian yeasts, especially saison yeasts. The carbonation is excellent, and the flavor profile is complex, with citrus-like hops, rose hips, orange peels, and peppercorns all making their presence felt, as well as the ubiquitous oak and Brett barnyard elements. At 8% ABV and 40 IBUs, *Love Buzz* scores a bit higher on drinkability than the 9%, 100 IBUs *Bitter Monk*. Time in the cellar will allow the Brett to continue its magic, drying out the beer and increasing the funkiness. I love saisons and this is a wonderful example of the style.

Galaxy White IPA: Pours a crystal clear pale gold into the glass, with a big, rocky white head. The spices added to the beer are evident in its nose, with the kumquats being especially noticeable. I also pick up the littlest hint of funk from the Brett. The beer is very light on the palate, with excellent carbonation and a very refreshing balance of bitterness and spiciness. The Brett again makes its presence felt on the finish, though it is still pretty subtle (at least until the beer spends more time in the cellar). An excellent example of the White IPA style. Fermented and aged in French Oak foudres, 7% ABV, 50 IBUs.

The Darkest Hour Imperial Stout: Aged in French oak pinot noir and rye whisky barrels, this is a 13% ABV, 40 IBU heavy weight. It pours opaque with a nice, persistent mocha colored head. The nose had lots of whisky and wood notes, mixed in with the roasted barley and malty sweetness - very rich and complex. On the tongue, it is more of the same, with a thick, chewy mouthfeel surrounding notes of dark fruit, chocolate, roasted coffee, oak, whisky, and wine, all in an intricate and complex dance across your taste buds. The finish is long and slow, with some alcohol heat at the end. This is a superb beer, one deserving of being savored in small glasses amongst appreciative friends.

Anadramous Sour Black Ale: 8.5% ABV and 30 IBUs, brewed with Brettanomyces, Pedioccocus, and Lactobacillus. It was then aged in over 40 French pinot noir wine barrels before being blended and bottle-conditioned. The beer pours opaque with a small tan head. The aroma is rich and slightly tart, with a touch of dark fruit; no Brett funkiness, at least at this stage, but some oak elements present. Not super sour at first taste, pleasant tartness and more oak, with medium mouthfeel and moderate carbonation.

A Deal with the Devil Barley Wine: This monster of a beer had an Original Gravity of 1162, resulting in an ABV of 17.3%, making it easily the strongest beer ever brewed in Alaska. It took over 4000 pounds of malt to brew this beer, and four separate 3.5-hour boils to fill just two 110-gallon used cognac barrels. It was brewed in February, 2012 and then aged in the wood for over 8 months. What's even more amazing is that this is a single malt, single hop beer, quite unusual for a barley wine. When released on draft only at the 2013 Great Alaska Beer & Barley Wine Festival, it easily walked off with first place in the barley wine competition. This is literally the finest barley wine I have ever tasted. You would believe that it is north of 17% alcohol. It is so smooth and deep that I would have guess more like 12% tops. It is incredibly complex, with a balance and depth of flavor profile that has to be experienced to be believed. Despite the challenges associated with brewing it, I sincerely hope this beer will be making an annual appearance and perhaps even migrate into a bottled version.

Distribution and Availability

Thanks to their distribution arrangements with Shelton Brothers, Anchorage Brewing Company's beers are available across the country and even in Europe. In Alaska, they are available at better bottle shops around the state, especially in the Anchorage area. Currently, they are not for sale at the brewery, since Anchorage Brewing Company has no public taproom.

Broken Tooth Brewing Company

Location:

2021 Spar Ave.

Anchorage, AK 99501

Phone: 907-278-4999

Email: brokentoothbrewing@gmail.com

Website: brokentoothbrewing.com

Hours of Operation: The brewery is not open to the public. Beers are sold at the Moose's Tooth Pub & Pizzeria and the Beartooth Theatrepub & Grill.

Driving Directions:

To Moose's Tooth Pub and Pizzeria: Travel north on the Old Seward Highway until it ends. Moose's Tooth is at 3300 Old Seward Highway.

To the Beartooth Theatrepub & Grill: West on Northern Light Blvd from the Seward Highway. Take a right on Spenard Rd. Left on W. 27th. Beartooth is on the left.

To the Brewery: From East 5th Ave/AK Route 1 in Anchorage, turn north on to Reeve Blvd (opposite Merrill Field). Take the third left on to Viking Drive, and then the first left on to N. Wrangell St. Take a right on to Spar Ave, and the brewery will be on the right.

Overview

The Broken Tooth Brewing Company came into existence in 1996 under the name Moose's Tooth Brewing Company. It was founded by Rod Hancock and Matt Jones under a brewpub license to supply beer to their newly-opened pub & pizzeria. Their undertaking was an immediate success and has expanded several times since, to include the Bear Tooth Grill and Theatre Pub. Today, the Moose's Tooth Pizzeria sells more pizzas than any other non-chain pizzeria in the US.

Since its founding, this endeavor has had substantial success at the Great American Beer Festival. Here is a list of the medals they have won:

2008 Gold Medal – Darth Delirium | Belgian-Style Strong Specialty Ale
2007 Bronze Medal – Smokin' Willie Porter | Smoke-Flavored Beer
2006 Bronze Medal – Bear Tooth Ale | American-Style Brown Ale
2005 Bronze Medal – Prince William Porter | Brown

Porter
2005 Bronze Medal – Pipeline Stout | American-Style
Stout
2004 Bronze Medal – Fairweather IPA | American-Style
Strong Pale Ale
2003 Bronze Medal – Prince William Porter | Brown
Porter
2001 Gold Medal – Darth Delirium | Chocolate/Cocoa
Flavored Beer

Head Brewer Tyler Jones, with Sean Heyer and Matt Turner

In early 2012, the brewery's name was changed to
Broken Tooth Brewing Company. This change was to
support their expansion into canned beers and to
establish an identity for the brewery separate from that
of the pizzeria. However, the brewery continues to
operate under a brewpub license, which limits total
production to 15,000 barrels annually for sale at the
three venues that are under the same ownership.

Broken Tooth can also sell a maximum of 1200 barrels annually to a distributor. Broken Tooth currently hits this wholesale cap every year, which is currently limiting their production.

Brewery Characteristics

The Broken Tooth brewhouse is a 30-barrel steam-jacketed system, from AAA Metal Fabrication. Batch sizes are typically 15, 30, or 60 barrels. Current annual production is approximately 6,000 barrels, out of a total capacity of approximately 15,000, for the reasons noted above. Most of this output is kegged, but two beers (*Chugach Session Cream Ale* and *Fairweather IPA*) are also canned, using a Wild Goose WGC-250 Canner. The brewery also has plans to add a 2-barrel pilot system before the end of 2013.

Restaurant Menus

As the name implies, most people visit the Moose's Tooth Pizzeria for its pies. But besides some 35 different specialty gourmet pizzas, there are also appetizers, soups, salads, and desserts on offer. There are also several gluten free offerings.

At the Beer's Tooth, the offerings run more toward gastropub fare, with gourmet burgers, sandwiches, Mexican and Italian entrees, as well as seafood and steaks on offer. There is also an extensive brunch menu, available until 3 PM.

The Brewer Speaks

Broken Tooth Brewing's Tyler Jones in his own words:

How did you become a commercial brewer?

Homebrewed deliciousness.

Right place right time. Keg clean grunt.

Still haven't quit yet.

What do you see as the biggest challenges facing a craft brewer in Alaska?

Shipping. Shipping kills. All ingredients need to be shipped up and fuel costs keep rising. That's a tough game to win. Thankfully, our water is great and we have plenty of it, which is not the case in some other parts of the country.

What characteristics do you think define Alaskan craft beer, as opposed to craft beer brewed elsewhere?

I've always found beer made in Alaska to be generally bolder than beer made elsewhere. Our IPA's are bigger and hoppier. Our Stouts are thicker. Even our smaller beers have more mouthfeel than beers made elsewhere. Maybe we need more calories to keep us warm.

Where do you think Alaskan craft brewing in general and your brewery/brewpub in particular will be in eight to ten years?

In general I see the potential for more breweries that serve their communities the way places like Homer and

Haines and Kodiak are served by their respective breweries.

As for the Broken Tooth, a lot depends on whether the State of Alaska ever changes the legislation that currently inhibits our growth. If the legislation gets changed, things can look very different. If not, we'll probably just make a lot more Root Beer!

The Beers

Regular Beers:

Chugach Session Cream Ale: 4.8% ABV, pours a clear gold with a nice, white head. The aroma is slightly nondescript, with malt notes mingling with a bit of hops. On the palate there are good, clean malt flavors that you typically get from this style of beer, nice carbonation, and just enough hop bitterness for balance. It is light, refreshing, and has good flavors, which is what you want in a good session beer. Available in cans or on draft.

Fairweather IPA: 6.2% and 64 IBUs. It pours a light copper color with a nice off-white head. The nose is loaded with hop aroma, distinctly Pacific Northwest in its piney, resiny character. In the mouth the bitterness is good, flavors were clean, and the beer is tasty. My only criticism is that the finish is a bit abrupt, but otherwise an excellent IPA. Available in cans or on draft.

Bear Tooth American Brown Ale: Light brown in color with a tan head and slight dry hop haze. More assertively hopped than many browns, its aroma is clean and citrusy with subtle malty sweetness. Its flavor is predominantly hop forward. At the start citrusy hop flavors blend with a dry, malty fullness. Malt flavors dominate the middle while a pleasant hop tingle lingers in the finish. 6% ABV, 39 IBUs. Draft only.

Hefeweizen: Refreshing and approachable, brewed with wheat yeast and unfiltered, this classic Hefeweizen style yields a pale yellow color a cloudy hue. Its aroma and flavor are an intriguing blend of yeast notes, wheat tartness and citric hoppiness. Try it alone, or pair it perfectly with a slice of lemon or orange. 5% ABV, 13 IBUs. Draft only.

Moonflower ESB: If you like hops this beer is for you. The aroma of dry hopped Challenger, the citrusy flavor of Cascade and the lingering bitterness of Chinook are all tied together with a firm malty fullness. 5.4% ABV, 31 IBUs. Draft only.

Northern Lights Amber Ale: A brilliant copper-colored ale with a slightly off white head. Its aroma is redolent of citrusy hops with caramel and toasty notes appearing as the beer warms. Caramel features prominently in its flavor, while the body is round and moderately dry. The hops play a supporting role in the flavor while keeping the caramel richness in check and providing a clean finish. 5% ABV, 15 IBUs.

Pipeline Stout: A full bodied, inky black American Stout. Its rich aroma showcases roasted and chocolate malt and is accentuated with a hint of citrusy, spicy hops. Its flavor features a luxurious maltiness with roast highlights that fades to a hop balanced, chocolate fullness. 6.3% ABV, 34 IBUs.

Polar Pale Ale: Honey-golden in color and capped with a persistent white head. Its aroma whispers softly of hops...in tones of apricot, citrus and spice. Dry and balanced in body, lots of late addition hops keep the bitterness down but the hop aroma and flavor high. It finishes clean and dry with the lingering interplay of mild malt body and citrusy dry hops. 5.2 % ABV, 17 IBUs.

Prince William Porter: A roasty, medium bodied, highly drinkable American Brown Porter. In the glass it is rich brown in color with ruby red highlights and a light brown head. Its aroma exhibits a malty blend of caramel and chocolate with hints of smoke and spice. Its body features a restrained maltiness supported by a subtle hop bitterness that finishes clean and refreshing. Despite its dark color this beer is very drinkable and food friendly. 5.1% ABV, 28 IBUs.

Seasonal & Specialty Beers:

Smokin' Willie Porter: A modified Prince William Porter recipe, this beer includes some grain cold-smoked over alder and apple wood, plus a dash of Victory malt for toastiness. The result is an award-winning Smoked Brown Porter. 6.0% ABV, 29 IBUs.

Darth Delirium Belgian Stout: This beer is a big, rich Belgian stout. Its full, roasty body gives way to a smooth chocolate finish. Winner of two Gold Medals at the Great American Beer Festival and a Bronze Medal at the World Beer Cup. 12.1% ABV, 85, IBUs.

Note: These are just two examples of the numerous specialty beers produced by Broken Tooth. In 2013 alone 47 different beers were brewed and released! In addition to unscheduled releases, Broken Tooth releases a new beer on the first Thursday of each month as part of its First Tap Party Series.

Distribution and Availability

Broken Tooth Brewing can be found most easily at the Moose's Tooth Pub & Pizzeria and the Bear Tooth Theatre Pub & Grill. You can find their canned beers for sale at those locations as well. Additionally, you may find some of the beers on tap around the state.

Glacier BrewHouse

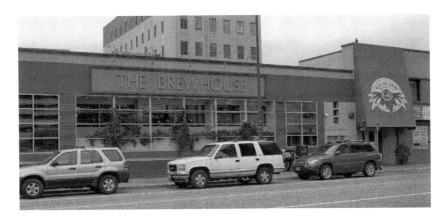

Location:

737 W 5th Ave, Suite 110

Anchorage, AK 99501

Phone: 907-274-2739(BREW)

Email: info@glacierbrewhouse.com

Website: www.glacierbrewhouse.com

Hours of Operation:

11 am to 9:30 pm Monday. 11 am to 10 pm Tuesday to Thursday. 11 am to 11 PM Friday. 10 am to 11 pm Saturday. 10 am to 9:30 pm Sunday.

Driving Directions: The brewery is in downtown Anchorage on the north side of West 5th Ave, on the block between G St. and H St.

Overview

The Glacier BrewHouse was established in 1996 by Chris Anderson and Bob Acree, and consistently ranks in the top ten of the 1200+ brewpubs in the United States in annual production. It holds a full liquor license, in addition to its brewpub license. It is consistently voted the best brewpub in Anchorage by local residents.

Brewery Characteristics

The brewhouse is a 15-barrel single infusion mash system. Glacier is most famous for its "Wall of Wood". In partnership with Barrel Builders, California's oldest continually operating barrel cooperage, Glacier developed an impressive collection of barrels in a chilled vault beneath the brewery. Among this wall-and-a-half of casks are at least fifty barrels of special release beers, conditioning in various types of oak that have been selected for the nuances each may impart. Virgin Oak infuses notes of vanilla and coconut on the palate. Those formerly used for Chardonnay or Jim Beam will pass on the distinctive characteristics of their "mother tongue" while conditioning. Hungarian, Ukrainian, and French oaks have their own distinctive profiles to add.

A small part of the Wall of Wood

The exceptional brews produced from the amazing selection of barrels are offered to best effect during the annual Twelve Days of Barley Wine, which runs each year from December 10th to the Winter Solstice on December 21st. Each day has four different high gravity beers on offer, including a daily cask offering.

Restaurant Menu

Besides its exceptional beers Glacier Brewhouse (and its next-door sister restaurant Orso) are renowned for some of the finest food in Alaska. Glacier is very much in the mode of a gastropub; you can expect some absolutely top-notch dishes on offer, such as dishes featuring Alaskan seafood (king crab, salmon, and halibut), dishes cooked of a grill fired with alder wood from Kachemak Bay, as well as brick-oven pizzas. Given their popularity with tourists and locals alike, it's often difficult to find a seat in either restaurant. Reservations are recommended.

Head Brewer Kevin Burton, with Bart Chelmo and Drew Weber

The Brewer Speaks

Glacier BrewHouse Head Brewer Kevin Burton in his own words:

How did you become a commercial brewer?

"Hard work, apprenticeships, and formal brewing education at the Seibel Institute in Chicago, Illinois. And more hard work."

What do you see as the biggest challenges facing a craft brewer in Alaska?

"Infrastructure for brewery utilities and brewer education opportunities."

What characteristics do you think define Alaska craft beer, as opposed to craft beer brewed elsewhere?

"The water. Cold weather."

Where do you think Alaska craft brewing in general and your brewery/brewpub in particular will be in eight to ten years?

"There is a glut of breweries right now just as in the 1990s. Some will survive and some will not. The difference now being that the beer is better quality. In the 90s, breweries failed due to bad beer and/or bad business practices. Today, most of those without business acumen will probably fail. It is much more of a competitive environment now. As for us, continued successful growth is predicted for the next ten years."

The bar at Glacier BrewHouse

The Beers

Regular Beers:

Blonde Ale: This is a crisp and refreshing blonde ale, with a nice aroma from Centennial hops and a smooth, creamy finish. Premium two row barley from the Pacific Northwest gives the beer a nice malt backbone. 4.76% ABV.

Amber Ale: Malty, medium bodied, with hints of chocolate and caramel from crystal malt, Munich malt, and roast barley. Nicely hopped using Cascades. 5.67% ABV.

India Pale Ale: Glacier uses a special double dry-hopping regime on this beer. Simcoe and Amarillo hops are added to both the aging tank and the serving tank, nicely compliment the floor-malted barley English barley used in this fruity, unfiltered, session–like IPA. 6.35% ABV.

Oatmeal Stout: Premium pale malt from the Pacific Northwest is combined with various dark and crystal malts and rolled oats to produce this silky and delicious brew. The smooth creaminess is enhanced by its being dispensed using nitrogen. 5.61% ABV.

Bavarian Hefeweizen: Usage of genuine Bavarian yeast produces the classic fruity aromas of banana and clove. This beer is brewed using premium German pilsner malt and German Tettnanger hops, to produce a beer that's low in bitterness, refreshing, and smooth. 5.00%, ABV.

Raspberry Wheat Ale: This beer is loaded with Alaskan red raspberries, giving it a deep red color and fruity flavors. Tart and satiating. 4.76%, ABV.

Imperial Blonde Ale: The addition of honey is used to boost the alcohol level of this brew, while retaining the smooth, creamy mouthfeel of a blonde ale. 9.00% ABV.

Seasonal and Specialty Beers:

Cask conditioned ales: Glacier BrewHouse has a beer engine installed in their bar, allowing them to serve cask-conditioned brews in the proper manner. The beer on offer varies from day to day, so be sure to inquire.

Black Rye Bock: This dark lager combines the characteristics of three winter beer styles. All three of these styles traditionally come from the colder harsher areas of Europe. The styles are (1) Black Beer (aka Schwartzbier) originating from Bad Kostritz in Thuringia (former East Germany); (2) Rye Beer which at one time was only made in hardier areas of Eastern and Baltic Europe; and (3) Bock Beer which is widely known as the higher alcohol lager of Northern Germany. *Black Rye Bock* has a distinctive bitter chocolate palate and black color reminiscent of a black beer. The spiciness from the rye malt shines through in the flavor. The high alcohol balanced with malty sweetness rounds out this cold season bock. 6.50% ABV.

Big Woody Barley Wine: The star of the Twelve Days of Barley Wine Festival, this beer is available in numerous variations and vintages, depending upon what sort of barrel-aging it has undergone. Various versions have been aged in whiskey and wine barrels, so be sure to read the individual description. ABV varies, but is always equal to or greater than 9.0%.

Distribution and Availability

All of Glacier BrewHouse's production is draft beer, with about half of the beer produced being distributed to bars and restaurants across Alaska and into Washington by Odom Corporation. However, the rarer and limited production brews are typically only available at the BrewHouse itself.

King Street Brewing Company

Location:

7924 King Street

Anchorage, Alaska 99518

Phone: 907-336-KING (5464)

Email: info@kingstreetbrewing.com

Website: www.kingstreetbrewing.com

Hours of Operation:

3 to 8 PM, Monday thru Friday; noon to 8 PM on
Saturday. Closed on Sunday.

Driving Directions: From the Seward Highway in
Anchorage, head west on East Dimond Blvd. Turn north
on to King Street. The brewery will be about a quarter-
mile up on the left.

Overview

Anchorage, Alaska is a beer-loving town; there's no doubt about that. Still, given its relatively small size and the fact that it already had three brewpubs and two breweries, not to mention a strong presence by such established regional players as the Alaskan Brewing Company from Juneau, you'd need a fair degree of chutzpah to decide to jump into that market by opening yet another brewery. Fortunately, King Street Brewing Company founders Dana Walukiewicz and Shane Kingry have plenty of that.

Shane tells their origin story this way: "While I too had daydreamed of opening a brewery, the first time Dana suggested to me that we pursue this together, I just chuckled to myself and let it go. I did the same the next time he brought it up too. It was only when he suggested it a third time that I realized he was serious. We got busy planning King Street immediately, and things haven't slowed down since!"

Both men had been homebrewers since the mid-90s, but in early 2009 they started to work on their business plan in earnest, eventually signing a lease on their current location of 7924 King St. in September, 2010. Even before that, they had been searching to locate and purchase a suitable brewhouse. Initially, they were looking for a 3-barrel system, but later they decided that they needed a 7-barrel at minimum.

King Street Brewery, looking down from the grain loft

"We looked at several used systems, even flying down to the Lower 48 to check some of them out," said Shane. "The asking prices were relatively steep, and then there would be substantial shipping, installation and refurbishment costs on top of that. Plus there's always the risk that we'd be buying someone else's problems. In the end, we decided to go with a brand-new brewhouse, a 10-barrel system from Premier Stainless."

All the parts and pieces of the puzzle were finally in place by September of 2011, and King Street Brewing opened for business. Dana and Shane decided that their initial beer offerings would be interpretations of classic beer styles, adapted from their successful homebrew recipes. They even eschewed clever or catchy names, simply calling their first brews King Street

Blonde and King Street Stout; the idea was to let the beers speak for themselves.

And speak they did. The good people of Anchorage embraced King Street and its beers. In fact, Shane and Dana were so impressed with the response that they decided to create the Founding Residents Program only a couple of months after opening as a way to thank the community for supporting the brewery. For $200, members received a limited edition tap handle signed by the two of them, a special embroidered long sleeve shirt and hat, a pair of King Street pint glasses and premium newsletter status that gives them first notice of special events including exclusive first tapping of beers at the brewery. Also included was the "Golden Growler" program. Members received a limited edition growler that allows the holder to stop by the brewery for two years (through 2013) and receive growler fills of the beer of their choice for $5.

As it turned out, there was plenty of room for more good beer from another brewery on the Anchorage beer scene. "Our biggest surprise was the strength of the immediate positive response," said Dana. "We had thought we might need to purchase more tanks in a few years. Instead, we were looking to expand less than six months after opening." That expansion took the form of two additional 40-barrel conical fermenters that were added in the fall of 2012, increasing King Street's fermentation capacity from 60 to 140 barrels. This should allow them to keep up with demand, at least for the next year or two.

Brewery Characteristics

As mentioned above, King Street's brewhouse is a state-of-the-art 10-barrel system, manufactured by Premier Stainless. The addition of more conical fermenters in 2012 has increased their fermentation tankage to 140 barrels.

King Street's 10-barrel brewhouse

King Street also has a somewhat unique brewery layout, with its grain storage in a loft area. Pallets of grain can be moved by forklift to the loft, and then poured into the grain mill below, eliminating the need for malt to be moved by hand to be poured into the mill's hopper, a very common chore in many small breweries. This sort of foresightedness is characteristic of the entire King Street operation.

In the last year, King Street has begun to experiment with aging beers in used whiskey barrels, as well as canning their beers using a manual two-head canning machine from Cask Systems.

The Brewer Speaks

Dana Walukiewicz and Shane Kingry of King Street in their own words:

How did you become a commercial brewer?

...with pure ambition and a bit of naivety. We began King Street Brewing Company with absolutely no commercial brewing experience. It started about five years ago when Dana was over at Shane's house during one of his infamous 4th of July BBQ's, and Dana found out that Shane was a homebrewer. Being a fellow homebrewer himself for nearly 15 years, Dana mentioned, "I've always wanted to start a brewery." That started the ball rolling, and it keeps on rolling today.

What do you see as the biggest challenges facing a craft brewer in Alaska?

Sadly, regulation is a big challenge. On top of logistical challenges of brewing outside the Continental United

States, breweries are regulated by multiple entities at the federal, state and municipal level, each with its own rules, or in some cases, differing or ambiguous interpretation of the same rules.

Shane Kingry and Dana Walukiewicz

What characteristics do you think define Alaskan craft beer, as opposed to craft beer brewed elsewhere?

As a generalization, Alaskans aren't exactly conformists, and their brewers tend to follow suite...or...not as the case may be. If there is some sort of locally indigenous ingredient available in the state (including native yeast), it's likely to have been put in a beer, most oftentimes with great effect! Alaskans are also born travelers, and as such, bring new (or even old) ideas from distant lands that help to inspire the brewers here to create their vision of what the beer should be.

Where do you think Alaskan craft brewing in general and your brewery/brewpub in particular will be in eight to ten years?

Hopefully still on King Street! We opened two years ago and have been overwhelmed with the support from the local community. It's hard for us to imagine where that will take us, but for sure, we don't plan to alter the quality of the ales and lagers we produce. We have always strived to be accessible to our customers, and our recently added packaging venture has been a natural evolution of that. Alaskans' propensity for outdoor activities combined with the multiple merits of canning, made cans an easy choice. We plan to expand our canning offerings so others who are not able to come to the brewery can enjoy our creations as well. Many of the breweries in the state are young, and like us, will continue to grow into their full potential. A consistent, unique, and quality product will do well as Alaskans love their beer! The passion shown by the brewers is infectious, so expect to see Alaska's beers more prominently represented in the continental United States as well.

The King Street tap room

The Beers

Regular Beers:

Amber Ale: A rich and complex beer balanced more toward the malts with smooth supporting hop flavor. The hops provide pleasant citrusy notes in the aroma and flavor giving way to a subtle nutty character reminiscent of English ales. 5.1% ABV. Available in cans.

Blonde Ale: This malty temptress has an upfront biscuit aromatic flavor that grabs a hold of you and makes you thirst for more. Clean hops balance and support a full bodied finish. 4.9% ABV. Available in cans.

Hefeweizen: Organic wheat and German Pilsner malt burst with flavor and perfectly compliment the rich clove and banana aromas in this authentic German Wheat Beer. Unfiltered. 5.7% ABV. Available in cans.

IPA: A pronounced but pleasant tangerine and passion fruit aroma opens the door for a complex mix of orange, grapefruit, floral and spicy flavors that come in waves. This beer finishes clean and its medium body leaves you ready to enjoy another. 6.0% ABV. Available in cans.

Pilsner: This beer was crafted in the Czech tradition with a delicate hop aroma that is supported by a dry malt backbone and finishes with a clean hop balance...absolutely clear and beautiful. 5.5% ABV. Available in cans.

Stout: This modern take on the classic Irish Dry Stout is full of the flavors of roasted grain, chocolate and a hint of coffee without weighing you down. We serve samples and pints on nitrogen to enhance the creamy texture. 4.9% ABV. Available in cans.

Special Brews:

Irish Gael Export Stout: This is a stronger version of their Stout which has been aged in used whiskey barrels. It pours opaque with a nice tan head that dissipates to a collar. The nose is primarily of roasted coffee, but there are definitely some notes of wood and whiskey present. Mouthfeel and carbonation are good, and the flavor profile is smooth, rich and complex. The roasted malt flavors you expect from a stout are in the foreground, but you can also tell that there is a lot happening in the background, giving a lot of depth to the flavor profile. A very nice barrel-aged stout. 9% ABV. Available in bottles only.

Nobility Barley Wine: This English-style barley wine was aged for several months in used whiskey and chardonnay barrels before being bottled. It pours a very dark honey color, with a small cream-colored head that dissipates rapidly to a collar. The nose is of caramel and toffee, with hints of oak. The mouthfeel is good and the carbonation is moderate. The flavor profile is quite malt-forward, in keeping with the style, with elements of toffee and vanilla, quite rich and flavorful. It falls away gradually to a nice, long finish. 9% ABV. Available in bottles only.

Distribution and Availability

King Street Brewing's beers are distributed on draft throughout Alaska, though they are much more common in Anchorage and The Valley. Currently, their canned beers are only available at the brewery's taproom, select Brown Jug locations, Gold Rush Liquors, La Bodega Wine Beer Spirits, and Anchorage Wine House locations in Anchorage. They have released two beers in bottles, *Irish Gael Export Stout* and *Nobility Barley Wine*, which can be purchased at the brewery or at better beer stores in Anchorage.

Midnight Sun Brewing Company

Location:

8111 Dimond Hook Drive

Anchorage, AK 99507

Phone: Brewery 907-344-1179; Loft 907-344-6653

Email: info@midnightsunbrewing.com

Website: www.midnightsunbrewing.com

Hours of Operation:

11 AM to 8 PM, daily. Last call at 7:45 PM.

Driving Directions: From the Seward Highway in Anchorage, head east on East Dimond Blvd. Turn left to stay on East Dimond, as the main road becomes Abbot

Road. Take a left on to Petersburg Street and the brewery will be one block up on the right.

Overview

Founded in 1995 by Mark Staples and Barb Miller, Midnight Sun Brewing Company is the eldest of the breweries in Anchorage. Originally located is a small, cramped space on Arctic Avenue, next to a taxidermist, it moved to its current location in May, 2009. As part of this expansion, MSBC was able to open a combination restaurant/brewery taproom, known as The Loft.

Over the years, Midnight Sun has had several Head Brewers; here is the list, in chronological order:

- Ray Hodge
- Mark Staples
- Jimmy Butchart
- Kevin Burton
- Gabe Fletcher
- Ben Johnson
- Jeremiah Boone
- Lee Ellis (current)

Over its almost twenty years of existence, Midnight Sun has developed a reputation for brewing big, challenging beers, especially in the Belgian beer styles. From 2007 to 2010, Midnight Sun also brewed a yearly "Beer Series". These were several beers organized around a common theme. In 2007, the theme was "The Seven Deadly Sins". In 2008, it was "The Planets". In 2009, it was "The Crew Brews", with each employee designing a beer and appearing on the label. In 2010, the last series year, it was "Pop Ten". Since then, Midnight Sun has been revisiting the most popular beers from these years as part of "Alaska's Most Wanted".

In July of 2011, Midnight Sun also began canning their beers.

Brewery Characteristics

Since its founding, Midnight Sun Brewing Company has undergone several expansions, most notable when it moved to its current location in 2009. Besides this primary location, MSBC also rents a nearby warehouse which is used to house its extensive collection of barrels, as well as to store the mountains of cans needed to supply Alaskans' voracious appetites for their popular beers.

Midnight Sun's 15-barrel brewhouse in action

Midnight Sun uses a 15-barrel system from Specific Mechanical to produce its numerous brews. The brewery now has 475 barrels of fermentation capacity and 90 barrels of conditioning tank space. Additionally, it has over 140 wooden barrels at the nearby warehouse to support its extensive barrel aging program.

Typically, used whiskey barrels are employed to age big beers, such as imperial stouts and barley wines, while used wine barrels are employed for wild and/or sour beers. A 5-head automated canning line from Cask Brewing Systems is used to package canned beers, while a 4-head Merlin bottling line from Meheen Manufacturing produces 22 oz. bombers.

Restaurant Menu

The Loft's interior

Perhaps the nicest way to enjoy one of Midnight Sun's beers is in the brewery's taproom/restaurant, The Loft. Located on the second floor above and behind the brewery itself, The Loft is bright and cheerful, with a deck that provides excellent views of Anchorage during the summer. It is also the location for such events as First Firkin Friday, which involves the tapping of a cask-conditioned beer on the first Friday of each month, usually coupled with some sort of artistic event.

Visitors should be aware that The Loft is operated under Midnight Sun's brewery license; this means that by Alaska law, patrons are limited to 36 oz. per person per day for on premises consumption. The law also prohibits such amenities as bar stools or live entertainment. Given those limitations, The Loft is an excellent place to enjoy some of the eighteen MSBC beers on tap, either with or without food.

The Loft's serving counter

The food menu at The Loft is fairly eclectic, with daily hot specials and weekend brunches. Look for salads, soups, and sandwiches but expect them to be a cut above your typical bar/pub food. The Ancho Beef Dip, made from slow-roasted ancho chile-rubbed tri-tip, sliced and stacked on a fresh baguette and served with au jus and horseradish sauce is particularly excellent.

The Brewer Speaks

Midnight Sun's Head Brewer Lee Ellis in his own words:

How did you become a commercial brewer?

My brewing career began in my hometown of Redmond, Washington in 2002. I was a recently un-employed ski instructor and a friend recommended that I go apply at Mac & Jack's Brewery. I happened to walk in while they were shorthanded and was hired that day. I had been of age for just over a month and was in the very early stages of discovering craft beer. I had never home brewed or possessed an interest in anything more than drinking beer. It turned out that my mechanical, organizational, physical abilities were ideally suited for working in a craft brewery. I started out washing kegs and filling kegs, became a Brewer, then a Packaging Manager and now Head Brewer. It's kind of ironic that so many people imagine brewing to be their dream job while I never had any intention of making brewing a career, yet here I am 11 years down the road and loving every minute of it. Except for the minutes when I have to be up at 4 am to brew.

What do you see as the biggest challenges facing a craft brewer in Alaska?

To say any one issue is the "biggest challenge" would be tough to judge. Logistics are an obvious answer. Having to manage an international logistics chain is a never ending chore. The labor pool can be very shallow when it comes to qualified applicants as well. Brewing requires a very special skill set and the ability to be responsible about healthy consumption. In a state with so many jobs that pay very well and a small number of permanent residents, finding the right candidates can be challenging. The lack of qualified technicians for equipment repairs can also be problematic. From a sales stand point, Alaska can also be a difficult place to develop a loyal customer base due to the transient population of the Anchorage area. We have a lot of folks that come up from the lower 48 who are accustomed to their usual selection in the bars and liquor stores. Getting folks to stretch their tastes a little further can take a lot of work.

MSBC Head Brewer Lee Ellis at work

What characteristics do you think define Alaskan craft beer, as opposed to craft beer brewed elsewhere?

THE WATER! As the Olympia brewery logo used to say, "it's the water". Our brewing water in Anchorage is some of the best in the world. It is very soft and high in Calcium. The water is pretty much ideal for our wide range of Beers that MSBC produces. Creativity, Community, and Quality are adjectives that I think define the craft beer scene in Alaska as well. MSBC has worked hard for the last 18 years providing Alaskans with cutting edge beers that push the boundaries of style guidelines. I find that a number of other breweries around the state are producing beers that are more interesting than anything I have found around the lower 48. The Alaskan brewing community is an amazing group of folks to be a part of. There is a lot of information sharing, collaboration, and camaraderie. I have been around some other communities that were not nearly as positive and it has certainly made me thankful for the opportunity to be involved with the Brewers of Alaska. The quality of the beer in Alaska really stands out to me as well. I have had the opportunity to visit all but four breweries in this state and have never been disappointed. Being from the Northwest, I'm used to the "brewpub on every corner" situation. I experienced great disparity in taste and quality from one block to the next. I feel that Alaska brewers are more connected to their local communities and customers, giving them more incentive to ensure that their beer is better than good enough. Some brewers concern themselves with the opinions of internet reviews, while I find the opinions of my friends and neighbors to be of much greater importance. So I guess in summation, the Brewers themselves are what make Alaskan craft beer stand out amongst the American Craft Beer market.

Where do you think Alaskan craft brewing in general and your brewery/brewpub in particular will be in eight to ten years?

Hopefully booming! Unfortunately my crystal ball is in the shop so it is hard to say. I know there is a lot of talk about the impending collapse of the Craft Beer Market due to over-saturation and the increase in breweries making less-than amazing beers. It seems to me that Alaska will probably, just like the last recession, find itself immune to these issues for the most part. Although Alaska, as of 2012, is number four in the country for breweries per capita, I don't think we are seeing a "brewpub on every corner" scenario. It seems to me that Alaskan people are hungry for quality craft beer that is locally made. There have been several new breweries opening in the last few years, but I find that the majority of them are serving areas that needed a local brewery and were lacking. There are still many communities throughout Alaska that could support a brewery and do not have one. I hope to see more "bush" breweries serving the larger communities off the road system. MSBC has a bright future I believe. As long as we remain committed to quality and creating bold and awesome beers, the next ten years should be great. Humans have been loving beer since the beginning of civilization, so shall brewers flourish until the end of civilization.

The Beers

Regular/Year-round Beers

Sockeye Red IPA: Ample pale two-row malt creates a fresh, firm body while specialty malts impart a spawning red hue. The predominant hop character comes from Centennial, Cascade and Simcoe hops, giving this beer tremendous citrus and floral aroma and flavor. With 70 IBUs and an ABV of 5.7%, it's not too strong to enjoy a couple of these with dinner. It's got the big, hoppy bite you'd expect from a West Coast India Pale Ale, which can be too rough for some folks, who may be used to the more refined British or East Coast-style IPAs. Available in 22 oz. bombers, 12 oz. cans, and on draft.

Eighteen taps in The Loft at Midnight Sun

Kodiak Brown Ale: It pours a translucent ruby with a nice khaki-colored head. The aroma is an appealing mix of roast malt, caramel, and Pacific Northwest hops. Good mouthfeel, with the caramel malt leading the way, followed by nice, balancing hop bitterness from the Perle and Willamette hops. 5% ABV, 24 IBUs. This is a great, easy-drinking brown, perfect with a meal or as a relaxing choice after a hard day's work. Available in 22 oz. bombers, 12 oz. cans, and on draft.

Snowshoe White Wit: It pours an ever-so-slightly cloudy gold, with a decent white head that slowly dissipates to a collar. The aroma is full of spicy notes, both from the Belgian yeast used and from the coriander, cumin, and citrus peels added to the brew. The carbonation is nice, and the mouthfeel is light, making this an excellent summer refreshment beer. 4.8% ABV, 12 IBUs. Available in 12 oz. cans and on draft.

Oosik Amber Ale: Taking its name from the Inuit word for a club made from the fossilized penis bone of an extinct giant arctic walrus, this is a true German-style altbier, brewed with pale, Munich and crystal malts. Deep amber with copper highlights, this ale sports a toasted and caramel malt profile, balanced by traditional noble hops. A special yeast strain ferments this ale at cooler lager temperatures, giving it a smooth malt character and a clean finish. 5% ABV, 11 IBUs. Available on draft only.

Midnight Sun Kolsch: The brewery's nod to the novice craft beer drinker, this 5.0% ABV, 30 IBU interpretation of the classic German style is well-made and refreshing, with more noble hop aroma and flavor than you often find in American versions. Available on draft only.

Cans waiting to be filled

Panty Peeler Tripel: Midnight Sun's interpretation of this classic Belgian abbey style ale, the addition of Curacao (bitter) orange peel and coriander create a beautiful yet bolder tripel by infusing color, citrus and spice. At 8.5% ABV and 15 IBUs, you can understand how this brew earned its name. Available in 22 oz. bottles and on draft.

Monk's Mistress Special Dark Ale: Like **Panty Peeler**, this is an interpretation on another classic Belgian style, though in this case it is the dark strong quadruple, rather than the bright, golden tripel that serves as the inspiration. It's brewed with Belgian yeast, hopped with East Kent Goldings and Fuggles to 22 IBUs, and brewed to an impressive 11.5% ABV. It pours a very dark brown, almost black, with a good-sized tan head that is slow to dissipate. The roasted malts used give it a wonderful aroma, full of hints of dark fruits, like plums, figs, and raisins. On the tongue, the first thing you notice is a big alcoholic character, very boisterous and very warming. Mouthfeel is viscous, but the carbonation gives a lift, making it smooth and crisp. It's a very complex brew, and a great sipping beer. Available in 22 oz. bottles and occasionally on draft.

Fallen Angel Golden Ale: This Belgian-style golden strong ale was first brewed on June 6, 2006 (6-6-6). Its immense and immediate popularity lead to the creation of the Seven Deadly Sins series of beers for 2007. It was brewed annually for a June release, until 2012, when it was added to the year-round line-up. *Fallen Angel* has the lovely pale gold color and effervescent white head that you'd expect from a beer of this style. It's crisp and clean on the palate, with some light fruit notes that remind you that you're drinking an ale, rather than a lager. The 35 IBUs give just the right amount of bitterness, while the 8% ABV hides deceptively amongst all the flavor. Wonderfully brisk and refreshing, it's a great accompaniment to a good meal, or as an after dinner drink. Available in 22 oz. bottles and on draft.

Mammoth Extra Stout: This beer uses Pale Two-row, Special B, Biscuit, and Black malts, plus roasted barley. It's hopped with Magnum and Fuggles. It pours completely opaque with a nice tan head, just like a good extra stout should. The aroma is primarily roasty malt, but with some slight sweet chocolate notes. The head leaves nice lacing on the side of the glass. On the palate the mouthfeel is medium, not as thick and chewy as some heavy stouts. Malt flavors forward, both roasty and some sweetness, balanced with some citrus notes from the hops. Toward the end the hops get a bit more earthy (the Fuggles, I'd think) and the beer finishes nicely. Quite drinkable for its strength and style, at 7.8% ABV and 50 IBUs. Available in 22 oz. bottles.

Seasonal and Specialty Beers

XXX Black Double IPA: Originally brewed in 2009 to celebrate Specialty Imports' 30th Anniversary, *XXX Black Double IPA* is now produced each winter as one of MSBC's four "seasonal double IPAs". It pours very dark with some ruby highlights and a small tan head. The aroma is primarily hops, with no evidence of roast malt. On the palate there is a nice, balanced hop flavor; it actually does not seem to taste bitter enough to be 87 IBUs. Very nice and drinkable, even at 8.5% ABV. Available in 22 oz. bottles and on draft, January thru March.

Meltdown Double IPA: With the coming of spring, this DIPA backs down a bit on both the alcohol and bitterness, coming in at 8% and 80 IBUs, respectively. Available in 22 oz. bottles and on draft, April thru June.

Hop Dog Double Wheat IPA: At 8% ABV and 100 IBUs, this beer packs quite a punch, both in terms of alcohol and hoppiness. It pours a nice amber-gold, with a nice white head. The aroma is full of citrus notes, either from the hops, the wheat, or both. On the palate there is a bit of tartness from the wheat, along with a ton of bitterness from the massive amount of hops used. It finishes nice and dry, very refreshing. This is a nice summer quencher for folks who are crazy about hops. Available in 22 oz. bottles and on draft, July thru September.

CoHoHo Imperial IPA: Originally created at the request of Humpy's Alaskan Alehouse as an imperial version of *Sockeye Red IPA*, this beer is the best of the seasonal DIPAs, in my opinion. It weighs in at a hefty 8.0 ABV and 85 IBUs, as compared to *Sockeye Red's* 5.7% and 70. The brewers achieve this increase in strength by adding fun stuff such as brown sugar, maple syrup, honey, and juniper berries. The same hops are used (Centennial, Cascade, & Simcoe) but at a more generous rate to balance the heftier grain bill. The end result is an exceptional beer, with a wonderful mouth feel and a massive hop bitterness and aroma. This beer is a wonderful drink on a long, snowy evening by the fire. Available in 22 oz. bottles and on draft, October thru December.

Arctic Devil Barley Wine: This is an English-style barley wine. It is brewed once a year then aged in oak barrels for several months before the entire batch is blended, bottled and released. *Arctic Devil* is released once a year in January, to coincide with the **Great Alaska Beer and Barley Wine Festival**. Over the years it has earned numerous awards, including medaling at the **Great American Beer Festival** and First Place at both the **Toronado** and **Hard Liver Barley Wine Festivals**. Here is a review of the 2013 vintage: It pours a dark honey color with ruby highlights and a small, cream-colored head that dissipates quickly to a collar. The aroma is strong in malt, woody notes, and a touch of alcohol heat. The flavor profile is deep and complex, with notes of brown sugar, molasses, toffee, oak, and some alcohol heat on the long, rich finish. At 13.2% ABV and 20 IBUs, this is easily one of the best barley wines on the market. Available in 22 oz. bottles and limited draft, January release.

A portion of MSBC's barrel collection

Berserker Imperial Stout: A huge beer at 12.7% ABV and 30 IBUs, this brew comes to the table after aging in bourbon barrels. It pours opaque with no head to speak of. The aroma is of chocolate, coffee, and alcohol. Mouthfeel is good, but carbonation is quite low. The flavor profile is rich, deep, and complex, with notes of chocolate, coffee, molasses, and vanilla, falling away to a long, lingering finish. This beer is certainly a sipper, one to be shared with friends and savored long into the evening. Available in 22 oz. bottles and very limited draft, October release.

T.R.E.A.T. Imperial Chocolate Pumpkin Porter:
Winner of a Gold Medal at the 2007 **Great American Beer Festival**. It pours completely opaque, with a nice tan head. The aroma leads off with roasted coffee & dark chocolate notes, followed by the pumpkin spices. On the palate there is excellent mouthfeel, with just the proper degree of chewiness. The flavor profile is very rich and complex; I pick up dark chocolate, roasted coffee, raisins, spices again, and a touch of alcohol from the 7.8% ABV. Available in 22 oz. bottles and on draft, September release.

Trickster Pumpkin Ale: When I first tasted *Trickster*, I initially thought that they had given me glass of *Panty Peeler* by mistake. Then the differences started to kick in, with subtle, nuanced flavors of pumpkin, allspice, ginger, and black pepper. 7% ABV, 22 IBUs. Available in 22 oz. bottles and on draft, September release.

Distribution and Availability

Midnight Sun's beers are distributed by Specialty Imports and are widely available around the state, in both cans, 22 oz. bombers, and on draft. Most of their beers are also distributed in Washington, Idaho, Oregon, California and New York City.

Snow Goose Restaurant/Sleeping Lady Brewing Company

Location:

717 W 3rd Ave

Anchorage, AK 99501

Phone: 907- 277-7727

Email: gregthebrewer@gmail.com

Website: www.alaskabeers.com

Hours of Operation: Winter hours: Sunday to Thursday, 4 to 9 PM. Friday & Saturday, 4 to 10 PM. Summer hours: 11 am to 11 pm, daily.

Driving Directions: The brewery is in downtown Anchorage on the north side of West 3rd Ave, on the block between G St. and H St.

Overview

The Snow Goose Restaurant and Sleeping Lady Brewing Company (hereafter shortened to Sleeping Lady for ease of writing) is one of the oldest brewpubs in Anchorage, having opened for business in 1996. It has one of the nicest views in Anchorage from the deck of its upstairs pub, looking out on its namesake, Mt. Susitna, AKA The Sleeping Lady. On a clear day, you can even see Mt. McKinley in the distance to the north.

Greg Mills, Head Brewer

Sleeping Lady's beers have earned many brewing awards over the years, including:

Urban Wilderness Pale Ale won Silver Medals at the World Beer Cup in 2000 and 2002, and a Bronze Medal at the 2006 World Beer Cup.

Frozen Kriek won a Silver Medal at the 2010 World Cup.

10-barrel brewhouse from JV Northwest

Old Gander Barley Wine won a Gold Medal at the 1999 Great American Beer Festival and Silver Medals at the 2007 Great American Beer Festival and the 2008 & 2009 Great Alaskan Beer & Barley Wine Festivals.

Portage Porter won a Silver Medal at the 1998 Great American Beer Festival.

Urban Wilderness Pale Ale earned Silver Medals at the 1998 & 2002 Great American Beer Festival.

Brewery Characteristics

Sleeping Lady uses a 10-barrel brewhouse manufactured by JV Northwest Inc. It is a two vessel system, with a gas-fired brew kettle and a single-infusion mash tun. Total fermentation capacity is 75 barrels, with one 5-barrel, one 20-barrel, and five 10-barrel vessels. There are also seven brite tanks. Annual production is approximately 1000 barrels. Note also that Gabe Fletcher leases time on this same brewhouse to produce Anchorage Brewing Company beers, before gravity draining the fresh wort down to his brewery to begin fermentation. See the Anchorage Brewing Company section for more details.

The pub is also equipped with a hand pump, allowing cask-conditioned versions of its beers to be offered. The beer on offer varies, so be sure to ask your server. At any one time, there can be up to thirteen different beers on offer, plus a root beer.

Restaurant Menu

The food on offer in both the ground floor restaurant and the pub upstairs could best be characterized as "good bar food with an Alaskan twist." Several of the menu items highlight local ingredients, like the Caribou Meatloaf or the Mixed Alaskan Grill, consisting of salmon, cod, and reindeer sausage, skewered, seasoned and grilled. There are also salads, burgers, and pizzas available.

Restaurant on the ground floor

The Brewer Speaks

Sleeping Lady Brewer Greg Mills in his own words:

How did you become a commercial brewer?

I became a brewer in a very non-direct fashion. I, and some college friends, dabbled in home brewing in the late 90's. It wasn't fancy and it wasn't hard and it made a somewhat drinkable beer. Eventually, the local brew shop went out of business and we all turned of legal age. I never thought about home brewing again; I definitely never thought that I could get paid to brew beer. I spent my entire life yearning to be a medical doctor and went on to earn a handful of various degrees at the College of Charleston in South Carolina. I had begun to make the necessary preparations for entrance into medical school when the unimaginable happened: I no longer wanted to pursue medicine. I was happy and sure of my decision, but was completely lost like so many post-graduates of my generation. For the next few years, I played competitive rugby and worked as a carpenter (listed in order of importance). The rugby was great but the job lost its luster and I was at a loss, again. I spent an evening drinking beers and discussing the future with Andy, my brother. We realized that my favorite things in life were science and beer. This led to an internet search for "science and beer". The result was the Master Brewers Program and the University of California, Davis. I applied immediately, but told no one. My acceptance call came in the winter of 2006. The following day, I gave my notice and started dreaming of California. The programs at Davis were amazing. I met incredible people and was taught by legends of brewing science. I decided that I wanted to brew on a small scale in a situation where I could influence the recipes. My job search focused on brew pubs in interesting places. I found my home at Sleeping Lady in June of 2007.

What do you see as the biggest challenges facing a craft brewer in Alaska?

There are many challenges facing the brewers of Alaska. The biggest, of course, is cost. We have to ship everything to Alaska which is expensive and often slow. Predictions for grain usage are made months in advance to account for the delay in shipping. We also deal with seasonality and tourism. The population of Alaska more than doubles during our few months of summer. The brewers must produce beer that high in quality but in much larger quantities. The best challenge is one that we as local brewers created for ourselves. The clientele craves the new and exciting. We must keep our standard beers appealing while creating one-offs and seasonal beers that keep our customers happy.

What characteristics do you think define Alaskan craft beer, as opposed to craft beer brewed elsewhere?

I don't know what exactly separates Alaska beers from the rest of the world, but I know that we are fortunate. There are so many breweries making great beer and so many people willing to support us. Alaskans truly value local products.

Where do you think Alaskan craft brewing in general and your brewery/brewpub in particular will be in eight to ten years?

I am sure that there will be many changes in the next decade for craft beer. There will be breweries that fail, both local and worldwide. But, there will be many breweries that continue to grow and inspire new breweries to start. People love beer.

The Beers

Regular Beers:

Gold Rush Golden Ale: This beer is brewed with pilsner malt and noble hops from Germany, producing a smooth unfiltered ale that is as light and crisp as the finest pilsner.

Urban Wilderness Pale Ale: This ale is brewed with English malt, American hops and Alaskan water. It offers an excellent balance between bitterness and full malt flavor.

The pub upstairs

Fish On! IPA: A classic West Coast IPA, this beer is lighter in color, crisper, and much hoppier than IPAs in other parts of the country. It has a very dry finish and an intense hop aroma and bitterness. Its signature flavors come from using both Simcoe and Amarillo hops, which lend a very powerful, yet drinkable, bitterness and flavor.

49'er Amber Ale: The recipe for this ale includes malts and hops from North America and Europe. The beer is pleasantly hoppy in both the aroma and taste. The malt character is slightly sweet with toasty undertones.

Bravehart Scottish Ale: This beer is rich with a smooth malty flavor. A brown sugar flavor is achieved by scorching the wort during a two-hour boil. A single addition of Magnum hops lends subtle hop bitterness to balance the rich malt flavors.

Portage Porter: A dark chocolate colored ale with a blend of toasty malt flavors and caramel, this is a malt lover's paradise. Its rich flavor can allow you a glimpse into the history of how beer used to taste back in the 1800s.

John Henry Oatmeal Stout: This ale is as black as the Alaskan winter nights. Fuller in flavor and with a silky mouth-feel from the oats, the addition of a small portion of rye lends a spicy note. Conditioned with nitrogen, this stout pours with a frothy head and smooth feel.

Seasonal and Specialty Beers:

Old Gander Barley Wine: This vintage beer is aged in rye whiskey barrels. The aroma contains hints of vanilla, sugar and toffee. The hop bitterness is barely noticeable, but only so much as to counter-act the maltiness. The flavors are unique to a beer that spends so much time in an oak vessel.

Susitna Hefeweizen: The beer is produced according to classic German brewing traditions, using about 60% wheat in the grain bill. It is fermented with a very famous German yeast strain, producing aromas of banana and clove.

Distribution and Availability

In the past, Sleeping Lady has canned small amounts of their Urban Wilderness Pale Ale. However, currently all of their production is being kegged. While some of their beer is distributed, the best selection is available at the Snow Goose Pub located directly above the brewery.

Breweries in the Valley & on the Parks Highway

Arkose Brewery

Location:

650 E. Steel Loop

Palmer, Alaska 99645

Phone: 907-746-BEER (2337)

Email: info@arkosebrewery.com

Website: www.arkosebrewery.com

Hours of Operation:

2 to 8 PM, Tuesday thru Friday; noon to 8 PM on Saturday. Closed on Sunday & Monday.

Driving Directions: From the South Glenn Highway (AK Route 1), head east onto E. Inner Springer Loop. Continue straight for about one mile, until the road becomes E. Outer Springer Loop. Take a right onto South Eklutna St. Take the second right onto E. Steel Loop. Continue around the loop and the brewery will be on the right.

Overview

Arkose Brewery opened on October 11, 2011, the brainchild of the husband and wife team of Stephen and June Gerteisen. Stephen is a graduate of the U.C. Davis Master Brewers Program, while June has completed the Siebel Technology Institute Sensory Beer workshop and Beer Judging Certification program. He handles the duties of Head Brewer, while she serves as Creative Director, including producing their logo, marketing materials, and all their visual designs. June also offers special events at the brewery such as "Beer Meets Chocolate" and "Beer Meets Canvas."

Arkose Brewery focuses on producing classic beers styles that are inspired by nature, art, music, and all things creative.

Brewery Characteristics

The brewhouse at Arkose is a 7-barrel, direct-fired, single infusion system, purchased new from Metalcraft Fabrication in Portland, Oregon. Total fermentation capacity is 28 barrels, supplying six taps in the brewery's taproom, The Growler Cache.

Most brews are fermented using White Labs Pacific Ale Yeast (WLP0041), which leaves a nice malty profile and plenty of fruity esters in their beers. The only one of their beers not brewed with this yeast is their *New Colony Hefeweizen* (see below), which uses a Bavarian yeast to produce the classic banana & cloves flavor profile.

The Brewer Speaks

Brewer/Owner Stephen Gerteisen in his own words:

How did you become a commercial brewer?

"I became a commercial brewer, because I didn't have passion in my career in the medical field, but I was a passionate home brewer. I put two and two together and realized that brewing was my calling. I am fascinated with the science of brewing and with a biology degree under my belt and a year working in a brewery, June and I headed out on the Alcan to attend the 6 month long UC Davis Master Brewers program in California. On our drive back, we began planning our own brewery. Five years later our dream came to fruition in October 2011."

What do you see as the biggest challenges facing a craft brewer in Alaska?

"The biggest challenge facing brewers in Alaska is by far the shipping costs, finding an appropriate location, and the great distances between populated areas."

What characteristics do you think define Alaska craft beer, as opposed to craft beer brewed elsewhere?

"Brewers in Alaska are just as independent as the state itself. We embrace the challenge with innovation and creativity. We also support our community through beer-related events, ongoing "beerducation," and fund-raising with non-profits."

Stephen and June Gerteisen

Where do you think Alaska craft brewing in general and your brewery/brewpub in particular will be in eight to ten years?

"Craft brewing in Alaska will continue to grow and thrive and we will continue to grow and thrive as well. Our connection to the community strengthens every day and we will continue to pour our passion and creativity into producing quality craft beer that our customers have come to expect and appreciate. At Arkose, "Beer Matters" and we "Love Ales"!"

The Beers

Year-round Beers:

Bitter Earth ESB: Deep copper in color, light bodied, and a flavorful earthy session beer with a complex malt profile and pleasing hop bitterness. 5% ABV, 26 IBUs.

Steed Rye IPA: A lively spirited American Rye IPA featuring Magnum hops. Refreshingly rich and spicy with plenty of hop aroma and flavor. 5.5% ABV, 70 IBUs.

Boxcar Porter: Roasted and caramel flavors are balanced with the delicate influence of three hop varieties. Dark in color, hold it up to the light and take in the ruby hues. 5.3% ABV, 25 IBUs.

Spindrift IPA: English Maris Otter malt and three specialty malts firmly support this hoppy ale. Dry hopped with Cascade hops for an extra hoppy sensation. 5.5% ABV, 93 IBUs.

The tap room at Arkose Brewery (photo courtesy of Arkose)

Seasonal & Special Brews:

Maiden Mild Ale: A Spring Seasonal, this ale is auburn in color and gentle in taste and aroma with just enough sweetness to make it a refreshing session ale. 4.3% ABV, 11 IBUs.

New Colony Hefeweizen: A spicy and smoky ale with a hoppy tang. This brew features the late addition of German Northern Brewer hops. 4.1% ABV, 23 IBUs.

Blue Skies Organic Ale: Brewed each September to celebrate the anniversary of the brewery opening, this beer features organic 2-row malt, organic flaked barley and organic Fuggles hops. Balanced with subtle fruit and hop flavors, it finishes with a crisp and clean taste. 5.7% ABV, 16 IBUs.

Arkose Olde Colony Winter Ale: This beer is brewed in the winter during the Old Colony Days event in Palmer, Alaska. This dark roasty ale is infused with a hint of traditional holiday spices. The luscious coffee and chocolate aromas are sure to warm the cockles of your heart. 8% ABV, 28 IBUs.

Distribution and Availability

Arkose Brewery does not currently bottle or can, but you can find their beers at the brewery taproom and on draft at various locations throughout Alaska.

Last Frontier Brewing Company

The owners of Last Frontier Brewing did not responded to repeated requests to participate in this book project. Therefore there are no pictures of this brewpub, no responses to the brewer questions, and the author received no feedback from them on the below statements.

Location: 238 N Boundary St

Wasilla, AK 99654

Phone: (907) 357-7200

Email: lfbrew58@gmail.com

Website: http://lastfrontierbrew.com/Home_Page.html

Hours of Operation: Mon - Thu: 11:00 am - 9:00 pm. Fri - Sat: 11:00 am - 10:00 pm. Sun: 11:00 am - 9:00 pm.

Driving Directions: Travelling north on the Parks Highway from Anchorage through downtown Wasilla, The Last Frontier Brewing Company is located on the right-hand side in the block before Main St. It is across the highway from the historic train depot.

Overview

The Last Frontier Brewing Company opened in early 2011. It occupies the same location and uses the brewing equipment of the defunct Great Bear Brewing Company. Great Bear was the first brewpub to open in the Valley and was very popular for several years, until a dispute between the owners (rather than any business or brewing issues) lead to its demise.

In 2010, Randy Martin and his son Robby acquired the property and with the help of veteran Alaska brewer Ray Hodge were able to restore the brewery and reopen. Hodge trained Robby for several months on the job, until he was ready to assume the duties as head brewer.

Brewery Characteristics

No details on this facility are available.

Restaurant Menu

Last Frontier Brewing offers an extensive lunch and dinner menu. It serves certified Angus burgers and fresh-off-the-boat seafood. Its steaks and prime rib are Choice-grade. It also incorporates its brews into many items on the menu, e.g. *24 Karat Gold Lager* in its beer-battered halibut. There is an extensive appetizer menu, a large selection of soups and salads, hand-pressed burgers, chicken breast sandwiches, steaks, seafood, pasta, and gourmet pizzas.

The Beers

24 Karat Gold Lager: A German Helles, or golden lager, lightly hopped with German noble hops, delicious and balanced with a malty finish and a mild lingering hop flavor. 5.0% ABV, 21 IBUs.

Black Diamond Dark Lager: A German Schwarzbier with a full bodied malty profile of roasted and toffee flavors balanced with just enough hops to provide a rich and robust flavor. 4.2% ABV, 30 IBUs.

Gold Dust Maibock: A German strong beer, made with Munich and caramel malt, balanced with just enough hops to make this a malty lager with caramel color and a big beer flavor. 7.5% ABV, 26 IBUs.

Heavenly Wheat Ale: A light, malty American wheat ale, cold fermented for a soft and delicate flavor, subtly hopped with American noble hops and dry hopped for distinctive flavor. 4.7% ABV, 22 IBUs.

Prospector Pale Ale: A classic English pale brewed with North American and British malts, distinctively hopped to make this beer memorable and delicious. 5.0% ABV, 34 IBUs.

Imperial Topaz Amber Ale: Our Scottish amber ale is brewed with 2-row and roast barley using a single noble British style hop to create a unique and malty flavor. 5.5% ABV, 25 IBUs.

Garnet IPA: Brewed with British and North American malts this English style India Pale Ale is full bodied, rich in malt flavors and generously hopped for a distinctive hop flavor and aroma. 6.3% ABV, 53 IBUs.

Grubstake Stout: Brewed in the British tradition with lots of roasted malt character and hopped with enough noble hops to give this ale a rich, balanced and deeply complex flavor. 5.4% ABV, 48 IBUs.

Double Shovel IPA: This Double India Pale Ale is brewed with floor malted British Pale Malt, is full of Northwest Hops, and is fermented with highly efficient yeast to give it a big flavor. 5.4% ABV, 69 IBUs.

Motherload Barley Wine: Brewed with lots of British Pale Malt and enough hops to make this the most sensational beer on offer. Cellar aged for months for a big and bold taste.

Gold Digger Doppelbock: This is another German-style lager, brewed using Vienna and Munich malts and with just enough hops to make a strong malty beer with big flavor.

Distribution and Availability

Last Frontier beers are available on draft and in bottles at the brewpub in Wasilla.

Denali Brewing Company

Location:

Downtown location/Twister Creek Restaurant:

 13605 E Main Street, Talkeetna

Production Brewery

 Milepost #2, Talkeetna Spur Road

Phone: 907) 733 - 2536

Email: sassan@mtaonline.net

Website: www.denalibrewingcompany.com

Hours of Operation: Downtown location: Noon to 8 PM, seven days a week. Production Brewery: Not yet open to the public.

Driving Directions: Take the Talkeetna Spur Road off the Parks Highway. The Production Brewery will be on the right at Milepost #2. Continue on the Spur Road until you reach downtown Talkeetna. Take a left onto Main Street. The Denali Brewing Company & Twister Creek Restaurant will be two block down on the right.

Overview

Denali Brewing is the realization of a dream shared by its two founders, Sassan Mossanen and Boe Barnett. Mossasen was a successful building contractor and enthusiastic homebrewer living in the mountain town of Talkeetna. Barnett was teaching English at the University of Alaska Fairbanks, writing and publishing poetry, and home brewing in the Goldstream Valley outside of Fairbanks. The two future partners met over a keg of Barnett's homebrewed pilsner. Mossasen spoke of his passion for the community of Talkeetna whose proud, independent-minded citizens had, for years, been yearning for a brewery of their own. Barnett spoke of his desire to bridge the gap between beer geeks and regular folks who just like to drink beer.

Fast forward to July 11, 2009, and the opening of the Denali Brewing Company in downtown Talkeetna. The brewery began with a 10-hectoliter (approximately 8.5 barrel) system in a small space adjacent to the Twister Creek Restaurant, which Barnett and Mossasen are also part owners of. The brewery rapidly developed a statewide reputation for excellence and demand soon began to outgrow the relatively modest brewery.

Denali Beer Garden in downtown Talkeetna

In July 2011, Denali Brewing Company opened its much larger production brewery, located on the spur road leading from the Parks Highway into Talkeetna. One of the driving forces behind this expansion was Denali's decision to begin canning several of their most popular brews, joining a growing tide of craft brewers in the state who had chosen this form of packaging. The downtown brewery had a beer garden added to it, enabling patrons to enjoy their purchases outside. The opening of the production brewery allowed the original brewhouse to be used to produce batches of some of the more unique brews from Denali, while the larger facility supplied the demand for the flagship beers.

Brewery Characteristics

As mentioned above, Denali Brewing Company actually has multiple brewhouses under one umbrella. The original system is a 10 hectoliter system from Specific Mechanical. It includes a steam-jacketed tun, allowing for stepped mashes. Also crammed into the very small space in downtown Talkeetna are two 16-barrel and one 20-barrel fermenters, as well as six former whiskey barrels which are now being used to produce sour ales.

The original Denali brewhouse

Compare this small brewhouse with the production brewery, located outside of town. Here, Denali is using 30-barrel brewhouse from Allied Beverage Tanks to fill three 120-barrel fermenters, two 60-barrel fermenters, three 30-barrel fermenters, plus 120 barrels worth of brite tanks. The production brewery is also home to a 1-barrel Blichmann brewing system, which is used to pilot new beer recipes. Finally, a taproom is under construction at the production brewery, which when opened will offer twelve different beers on tap.

A big reason for the large size of the production brewery is to fill the great demand for Denali's flagship brews, four of which are available in cans. These cans are produced on a two-head automated canning line made by Wild Goose Canning Technologies Incorporated.

Restaurant Menu
While not an actual brewpub, Denali Brewing has a very close relationship with the Twister Creek Restaurant which is attached to its beer garden & downtown brewery. The restaurant's offering are uniformly excellent, and it tries to showcase local produce and seafood to the maximum extent possible. Typically, there will also be one or two Denali beers on offer in the restaurant which are not available at the beer garden next door. Finally, since the restaurant is not subject to the strictures of a brewery license, it can stay open longer and is not restricted in the amount of beer it can serve per person per day.

A sample of Denali beers from Twister Creek

Besides substantial appetizers and salads, choices on offer include craft sandwiches served on locally baked bread and a soup of the day. There are four different kinds of hamburger on offer, plus nine more specialty dishes, ranging from Cajun to Italian to Thai in their inspiration. Finally, there is a substantial dessert menu, including several created using various Denali beers. All these wonderful options make the Twister Creek Restaurant something not to be missed in Talkeetna.

The Brewer Speaks

Owner/Brewer Boe Barnett in his own words:

How did you become a commercial brewer?

Prior to starting Denali Brewing, I homebrewed for 10 years, always experimenting with and refining a small set of recipes. These recipes became the four standard Denali beers as well as a few of the other beers we brew.

What do you see as the biggest challenges facing a craft brewer in Alaska?

Distance from supply chains, logistics in general, distance to markets both inside and outside of Alaska, and the seasonal nature of Alaska (i.e., booming summers and winter slowdowns).

What characteristics do you think define Alaskan craft beer, as opposed to craft beer brewed elsewhere?

Alaska breweries were some of the early pioneers in what has become known as extreme brewing. I'm thinking in particular here of our friends at Midnight Sun. I believe those guys set the bar for what Alaska style brewing ought to be; that is, a solid core of very approachable beers surrounded by beers that are always challenging palates and pushing at the limits of accepted beer styles. It's refreshing to live in a state where style (with regards to beer and just about everything else!) does not dictate the landscape. Alaska is a land of free thinking and wild spirited individuals. We in the Alaska brewing industry are so fortunate that local beer plays such an important role in the lives of our friends and neighbors.

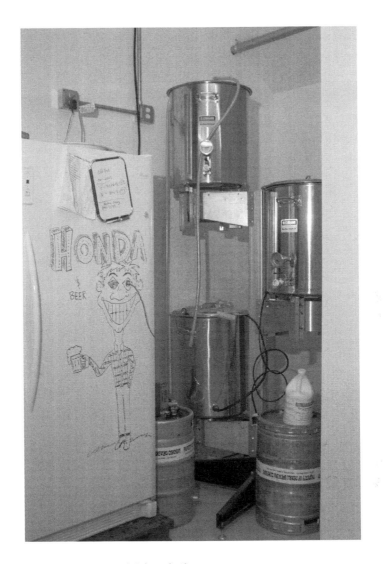

A 1-barrel pilot system

Where do you think Alaskan craft brewing in general and your brewery/brewpub in particular will be in eight to ten years?

Alaska will be home to at least 30 commercial brewing operations, be they production breweries, pubs or some combination of the two models. The quality of beer brewed in Alaska will continue to be excellent. We will continue to be on the forefront of exciting new industry trends and beer styles. The state will also become more of a destination location for beer tourism as beer travelers look to expand both their itineraries and their palates.

The Beers

Regular Beers:

Mother Ale: This rich-bodied blonde ale is smooth and satisfying. Brewed using North American pilsner and wheat malts, it's topped off with European noble hops. Very drinkable and refreshing. 5.6% ABV, 46 IBUs. Available on draft and in 12 oz. cans.

Single Engine Red Ale: This take on the classic Irish red ale style is brewed with five choice American and European malts and just enough hops for balance. Smooth, clean, and malty. 5.8% ABV, 46 IBUs. Available on draft and in 12 oz. cans.

Twister Creek IPA: The beer pours a clear, bright gold with a nice white head. It mixes British and American hops to produce an outstanding hop aroma and a very pleasing bitterness, but it still has a nice malt backbone to hang all those hops on. 6.5% ABV, 71 IBUs. Available on draft and in 12 oz. cans.

Chuli Stout: This brew is a foreign export stout and takes its name from the mighty Chulitna River. An ample amount of roasted barley imparts dry, coffee-like flavors, while flaked barley adds smoothness and body. Draft versions are conditioned and served using nitrogen, to increase the smoothness and producing the classic dense stout head. 5.9% ABV, 55 IBUs. Available on draft and in 12 oz. cans.

Fermenters at Denali's production brewery

Seasonal/Specialty Beers:

Denali Brewing produces numerous seasonal and specialty beers, so those listed are just a sampling. See their website for a more complete listing.

Flagstop Series: These limited edition specialty brews are bottled in 750ml corked and caged bottles. Each beer is in a different style and identified by a mile number.

Milepost #1: This beer is in the style of a Belgian Golden Strong Ale. It pours a deep, clear gold with a dense and slightly rocky white head, perfect for the style. The aroma had the peppery, spicy notes typically associated with Belgian yeast strains. Carbonation is excellent, and the mouthfeel is light and fairly dry. The initial impression is of clean, crisp bitterness, followed by some more spicy yeast notes, then a long finish with a touch of alcohol. 9.7% ABV.

Milepost #2: This beer is in the style of a Flanders Sour Red Ale. It pours a deep, clear ruby, with a massive off-white head. The nose has plenty of tartness, including some sour cherry notes. Carbonation is excellent and the mouthfeel is nice. The flavor profile is clean, with good lingering sourness on the finish. 6.6% ABV

Louisville Sour Ale: Produced in limited quantities using former whiskey barrels, this is blonde ale fermented in oak and dry hopped with a generous amount of Centennial hops. Look for flavors of tart apple, lemon, and grapefruit.

Whiskey barrels used for sour ales

Hibernale: Released around the winter solstice, this seasonal is Belgian-style Dark Strong Ale, with spicy notes from a blend of Belgian yeasts and plenty of malt goodness from dark crystal, Munich, and honey malts.

Abaddon: The summer seasonal counterpart to Hibernale, this beer is in the style of a Belgian Golden Strong Ale. It uses 666 pounds of pilsner malt and plenty of European hops to achieve an authentic Belgian taste.

Slow Down Brown Ale: Dark nut brown ale features velvety chocolate malt up front; a nutty center palate with restrained additions of cumin, coriander, fennel, fenugreek and cardamom; and a slightly sweet lingering finish highlighted by cinnamon, cloves and cayenne. This beer won Frist Place in the People's Choice Awards at the 2013 Mighty Matanuska Beer Festival, meaning it will be the official beer of the 2014 Alaska State Fair. Currently available only on draft, this will be the next beer to join Denali's line-up of cans, likely in mid-2014.

Distribution and Availability

Denali Brewing Company's regular beers are distributed widely around the state, in both cans and on draft. Specialty releases are typically only available on draft in Talkeetna, either at the Beer Garden or the Twister Creek Restaurant. Some of Denali's canned offerings have also been distributed as far as Washington, though in very small amounts. Denali has also produced specialty beers exclusively for the Tap Root Café in Anchorage.

49ᵗʰ State Brewing Company

Location: Mile 248.4 Parks Hwy.

Healy, Alaska 99743

Phone: 907-683-2739

Email: info@49statebrewing.com

Website: www.49statebrewing.com

Hours of Operation: Summer hours: noon to 1:30 am daily. Closed from late October to mid-April.

Driving Directions: Traveling north on the Parks Highway into Healy, 49ᵗʰ State Brewing will be on the right shortly after milepost 248.

Overview

Since opening in the summer of 2011, 49th State Brewing has experienced what can only be described as explosive growth. Its rapid expansion is even more remarkable when you consider that the brewery is only open for about half the year, from April to October.

Tourist in front of the bus used as a prop for Into The Wild

49th State Brewing is located in Healy, a small community on the Parks Highway, a few miles north of the entrance to Denali National Park. During the summer, the community is extremely busy, servicing the hordes of tourists who come to visit the park. During the winter, the park closes and the temperature dips to around -40 F along with plenty of snow, so it's easy to see why the brewery (along with many other businesses) goes into hibernation for the winter.

The brewery itself is located in a former bus barn and has a full liquor license. The outdoor beer garden in front of it is also home to a prop from the movie *Into the Wild*: a replica of the famous bus in which Christopher McCandless died of starvation.

Brewery Characteristics

When 49th State opened in 2011, their brewing system was a mere 1/3 barrel system, which could not even begin to keep up with demand. This small system did provide the opportunity to fine-tune recipes before moving on to a bigger system.

49th State's brewhouse

In June of 2012, 49th State began using its current 5-barrel direct-fired brew kettle and a mash tun with the capability to do true decoction mashes. Since then, the brewery has produced more than 150 batches and over

500 barrels of total production, supplying the brewpub in Healy and two restaurants, Prospector's Pizzeria and Alehouse and the Denali Salmon Bake. However, even this system has been unable to keep up with demand of all three locations, so the brewery plans to upgrade to a 15-barrel, three-vessel system in February of 2014.

Currently, 49th State has a total of 80 barrels of fermentation capacity, to supply 12 taps at the brewery. Over the winter from 2012 to the spring of 2013, the brewers decided to make a virtue of the necessity of shutting down. Just before closing for the winter, they filled every fermenter with beer that could benefit from a long, cold lagering, and then turned the heat down to just above freezing. This was the birth of their Hibernation series of beers, which were released upon the brewery's re-opening in April 2013, to wide acclaim. The experiment was so successful, that the brewery plans to repeat it each winter for the foreseeable future.

Restaurant Menu

The food at 49th State Brewing falls into the category of hearty Alaskan pub fare. There are heavy appetizers, such as wings, nachos, and chicken tenders, but also home-made pretzels and an excellent Back Country Platter of locally sourced salami, sausages, smoked salmon, pickled vegetables, and mustard. For soups, there is an exceptional beer and cheese soup, made from their *Baked Blonde Ale* and smoked gouda, or a dynamite Alaskan seafood chowder.

If you are there for lunch, look for some great burgers, all made from 100% premium ground chuck and quite big, along with a generous amount of fries. Or you can choose one of the several different sandwiches on offer, ranging from buffalo meatloaf to tundra grilled cheese.

At dinner time, the burgers and sandwiches are still available, but now you can choose from such additional hearty options as fish and chips, rib eye steak, or elk lasagna. There's even a limited Late Night Menu, served from 11 pm until closing time at 1 am. In short, you should plan to arrive hungry and leave full.

The Brewer Speaks

Brewer Jason Bullen in his own words:

How did you become a commercial brewer?

Back in 2005, I had just moved to California and while looking for work picked up a few shifts as a server at the local brewpub. Being in the restaurant, around all those shiny tanks and all that beer sparked an interest in me, so I decided to try it for myself at home. I quickly fell in love with the art and science that was involved as I delved further and further into the craft beer world. When I moved back to New York a few years later, I was lucky enough to secure an internship at Cricket Hill Brewery in NJ. After a few months I decided to pursue brewing as a career, and felt the best way was through schooling. I attended the Seibel Institute in Spring 2011, where I met David McCarthy, owner of 49th State Brewing Co. At the end of school, he gave me the opportunity to be the head brewer and start the brewing operations. I've been here ever since.

Head Brewer Jason Bullen

What do you see as the biggest challenges facing a craft brewer in Alaska?

Shipping and logistics are the number one challenge hands down. I would also say the limited amount of local ingredients available for the production of beer. The climate here is always going to limit what can be grown, but we have had good success using what we can get locally, like Birch Syrup, Honey, wild herbs, and such. Going forward we would like to incorporate as many different Alaskan ingredients as possible, because that is one of the biggest trends in craft brewing.

What characteristics do you think define Alaskan craft beer, as opposed to craft beer brewed elsewhere?

Community support for local beer in Alaska is outstanding. Because of how spread out Alaska's population is, it accounts for the success of more breweries than other parts of the U.S. The area I grew up in on the East Coast has a population roughly the same as the whole state of Alaska, but there is no way 20+ breweries would survive there. I think the uniqueness of Alaska's people in each specific region shines through in the philosophy and beer of each brewery and allows them to continue to thrive.

Where do you think Alaskan craft brewing in general and your brewery/brewpub in particular will be in eight to ten years?

The growth of the next generation of breweries is going to help move Alaska into the upper echelons of craft beer. For us at 49th State, it all begins with quality, education, and providing an unforgettable experience for the consumer. Constantly educating customers and staff a like about the history and culture of beer, as well as what outstanding, quality craft beer should taste like is paramount to pushing Alaska's beer scene to the forefront. Thousands of people from all over the world and all walks of life come to see Alaska and the beauty and wonder it has to offer. We want them to leave here when their journey is over, go back home, and tell people, "Damn, that place was incredible. I didn't know beer could taste that good." Rivaling the great beer meccas of the world, that's where we see ourselves in 10 years.

Flanders Oude Bruin sour ale aging in the wood at 49th State

The Beers

Baked Blonde Ale: This unfiltered golden ale has some fruit, floral and honey notes on the nose, with good malt sweetness and a clean hop flavor. Ingredients used include Munich malt, Cascade and Zythos hops. 5.6% ABV, 18 IBUs.

Solstice IPA: Big citrusy, piney, and juicy flavors highlight this well-balanced India Pale Ale featuring Columbus and Citra Hops. Ingredients used include crystal malt, with Columbus, Citra, and Cascade hops. 7.0% ABV, 65 IBUs.

McCarthy's Stout: This dry Irish Stout is a great session beer, with roasted barley and dark chocolate aromas, and a silky smooth finish. Served on nitrogen. Ingredients used include Maris Otter malt, flaked and roasted barley, with Magnum and Fuggles hops. 4.8% ABV, 35 IBUs.

Vienna Lager: An amber colored lager with a slight roasted nose, toasted malt and biscuit flavors, and a crisp, clean finish. Ingredients used include Bohemian pilsner and crystal malts, with Magnum and Saaz hops. 5.3% ABV, 30 IBUs.

The bar at 49th State Brewing Company

Dunkelweizen: A dark, unfiltered wheat beer in the traditional Bavarian style, with banana esters and clove highlights to go along with subtle caramel undertones. Ingredients used include wheat, crystal, and chocolate malts, with Perle and Tradition hops. 4.9% ABV, 15 IBUs.

Golden Dahl Tripel: This Belgian-Inspired tripel has lots of fruity esters and a subtle spiciness from the yeast that gives way to a warming alcohol finish. Ingredients used include Belgian pilsner, wheat, and aromatic Malts, Belgian candi sugar, with Northern Brewer and Saaz hops. 9.0%ABV, 19 IBUs.

Oatmeal Stout: This dark and roasty stout is full bodied, with a creamy mouth feel imparted by rolled Oats added to the mash. Ingredients used include Maris Otter, crystal, chocolate, and roasted malts, oats, and Northern Brewer hops. 5.2% ABV, 32 IBUs.

White Peach Wheat: Light and refreshing, this American-style wheat beer has white peach puree added during conditioning. Other ingredients used include: 2-row and wheat malts, and Warrior hops. 5.1% ABV, 15 IBUs.

Seasonal and Specialty Beers:

Equinox Double IPA: A bigger, bolder version of *Solstice IPA*, this beer more malt, more hops, and more punch. Ingredients used include 2-row, and crystal malts, along with Warrior, Columbus, Cascade, and Citra Hops. 8.8% ABV, 65 IBUs.

Pilsner: A soft malt palate blends seamlessly with the accompanying spicy hop bite to make this beer light, refreshing and enjoyable. Ingredients used include

Bohemian pilsner malt and Czech Saaz hops. 5.1% ABV, 40 IBUs.

Oktoberfest: Brewed once a year for 49th State's annual Augtoberfest, this crowd pleaser is malt, malt and more malt, crisp and clean. Ingredients used include German pilsner, Munich, and crystal malts, with Magnum and Tradition hops. 6.0% ABV, 29 IBUs.

The decor at 49th State is a bit unusual...

Chocolate Porter: Part of the Hibernation Series. Fair Trade cocoa nibs in the conditioning stage give this beer its chocolate flavor. Ingredients used include Maris Otter, wheat and roasted malts, along with Northern Brewer hops. 7.0% ABV, 30 IBUs.

Smoked Marzen: Part of the Hibernation Series. Brewed as an homage to the classic Rauchbiers of Bamberg Germany, this lager has an assertive, distinct aroma of campfire and hickory, with billowing flavors of sweet, smoky goodness. Ingredients include Munich, crystal, and smoked malts, plus Northern Brewer hops. 7.2% ABV, 29 IBUs.

Imperial Stout: Part of the Hibernation Series. This big black beer rests for almost 10 months before being unleashed. Roasted barley, chocolate, dark fruit, and port flavors are brought to life in this once-a-year beer. 9.0% ABV, 75 IBUs.

Wee Heavy Scotch Ale: Part of the Hibernation Series. This big Scotch Ale is all malt and full-bodied, with little hop character. Caramel and toffee notes abound, and the finish is soothingly warm. Ingredients include Maris Otter, Munich, crystal, and chocolate malts, plus Northern Brewer and Willamette hops. 8.0% ABV, 24 IBUs.

Vagabond Saison: Part of the Hibernation Series. This farmhouse ale is dry and effervescent with nice spiciness and a subtle fruity finish. Ingredients include Belgian pilsner and wheat malts, and Saaz hops. 7.4% ABV, 27 IBUs.

Hibernator: Part of the Hibernation Series. A true doppelbock, this beer is malty, complex, and strong. You will definitely be ready for a long winters nap after a few of these. Ingredients include German pilsner, crystal, and chocolate malts, along with Magnum hops. 6.7% ABV, 20 IBUs.

Distribution and Availability

Besides tasting 49 State Brewing Company's beers at the brewpub in Healy, you can also find them on tap at the Denali Salmon Bake Restaurant and the Prospector's Pizzeria & Alehouse in Nenana Gulch near the entrance to Denali National Park, since both those establishments and 49th State are under the same owners.

Fairbanks Breweries

HooDoo Brewing Company

Location: 1951 Fox Avenue

Fairbanks, AK

Phone: 907-459-2337 (BEER)

Email: greatbeer@hoodoobrew.com

Website: http://www.hoodoobrew.com/

Hours of Operation: Tuesday - Friday: 3pm - 8pm. Saturday: 11am - 8pm. Sunday & Monday: Closed. Free 30min brewery tours are available on Saturdays at 4pm. Sign up by phone or by asking in the taproom.

Driving Directions: Exit the Johansen Expressway in Fairbanks heading south on Peger Road. Take the first left, to head east on Phillips Field Road. Take the second left to head north on Olnes St. When Olnes St. dead ends in Fox Ave, take a left and the brewery will be immediately on your left.

Overview

HooDoo Brewing is the brainchild of Bobby Wilken, who along with four other family members opened the first brewery in Fairbanks since 1942. Wilken worked for five years at Alaskan Brewing Company in Juneau, learning his craft, before striking out on his own.

The HooDoo Brewing team

HooDoo Brewing seeks to produce classic beer styles, using genuine ingredients and authentic techniques. Their focus is almost exclusively on direct sales to the public via the brewery taproom, with no plans to expand their very limited availability on draft in

Fairbanks or to ever package their beers in bottles of cans.

Brewery Characteristics

The HooDoo Brewhouse tucks neatly into a corner

HooDoo Brewing uses a 15-barrel brewhouse from Premier Stainless, with a steam-jacketed kettle, a steam-jacketed mash tun, and a separate lauter tun, which facilities multi-step mashing. In Wilken's opinion, the ability to perform such a mash is a critical requirement to be able to produce proper versions of the classic German beer styles.

Currently, HooDoo has four 30-barrel fermenters and 2 30-barrel brite tanks. All beers are unfiltered and no finings are used.

Bobby Wilken

The Brewer Speaks

Owner/Brewer Bobby Wilken in his own words:

How did you become a commercial brewer?

When I walked into my first brewery in the late 1990's, I was awe struck. I remember asking with wide eyes how beer is actually made, and picking my jaw up off the floor when they finished their explanation - I was hooked. I started to absorb anything beer related. Books, magazines, breweries, and of course copious amounts of beer. The two main things I just loved about beer and breweries were the fascinating, age-old brewing process from grain to glass, and the wonderful social aspect of beer drinking with friends and family. There is nothing I enjoyed more than hanging out in breweries, so I did that any chance I could get. 10 years before HooDoo poured its first pint, I put myself (and my wife Jessica) on a mission to open our dream brewery in our hometown of Fairbanks someday. I homebrewed quite a bit, then eventually started working on a business plan. The project of opening a small brewery was daunting, so I eventually tabled the idea and went to brewing school in Chicago and Germany to learn as much as I could about the craft. I traveled around Europe and the US, making notes and talking to brewers about equipment, techniques, and ingredients. When I returned to Alaska I got my dream job as a brewer - and then eventually quality control - at industry pioneer Alaskan Brewing Company in Juneau where I got to experience the small brewery culture in all its glory. After four years with the great people at Alaskan, I came to a cross-road in my life. In the end, I decided to throw caution to the wind and venture back home to Fairbanks to start the small brewery I had been dreaming about for so many years. I quit the best job I had ever had, and dove in head first. Two years later, on Halloween 2012, HooDoo Brewing Company opened its taproom doors.

The HooDoo Mobile: a former German fire truck

What do you see as the biggest challenges facing a craft brewer in Alaska?

A few things come to mind. First, logistics are a constant challenge. We are thousands of miles away from our raw material suppliers, and the accompanying shipping costs reflect that. Second is extreme weather. We operate year round, and the -50°F temperatures we can see in the winter add an entirely new dimension to the logistical and mechanical challenges that are inherent in any brewery. And last, energy costs. Energy is very expensive in our part of the state and we have to be vigilant on how we use and re-use energy. The brewing process produces a significant amount of waste heat which we ravenously capture and contain to assist in a major expense to any Fairbanksan: building heat.

What characteristics do you think define Alaskan craft beer, as opposed to craft beer brewed elsewhere?

The overall quality of beers produced in Alaska is fantastic. Alaskans are quality driven, smart people, and will see right through any marketing campaign to convince you a beer is delicious when it is not. Quality and authenticity is paramount to the brewer in Alaska, and we all reap the benefits with great beer being brought to the table.

Where do you think Alaskan craft brewing in general and your brewery/brewpub in particular will be in eight to ten years?

We are witnessing a revolution of the brewing industry and beer consumers in this country. This is not a fad, and is in response to a real and significant shift in the American beer palate. This will become a worldwide phenomenon over the next decade. More and more small brewers are supplying fresh beer to their surrounding community, while at the same time providing jobs and a becoming part of the city's identity and culture. This culture of craft beer will continue to proliferate into smaller communities throughout the US, Alaska included. I love the idea of small communities with specialized, locally produced products. In general, any beer should be consumed as fresh from the brewery as possible, and locally brewed beer is as fresh as it gets. As far as where HooDoo will be in ten years...that is a long, long time from now. What I do know for sure is that we will be producing world class beer right here in the heart of Alaska. The quality of our beer and the satisfaction of our customers is absolutely our main concern, and will guide the course of our business for the next 150 years or so.

The Beers

Regular beers:

German Kolsch: HooDoo utilizes German malt, hops and brewing techniques to produce an excellent example of this classic style. The beer has a clean but complex malt base that marries perfectly with the delicate, subtle aromas of the noble hops from Bavaria. 5.3% ABV, 30 IBUs.

English Mild: Cask-conditioned and served via hand pump at cellar temperature, this is HooDoo's interpretation of this classic British session beer. Marris Otter malt is used to produce the delicious malt flavor that this style showcases, while the relatively low alcohol and natural carbonation leaves the drinker ready for another pint. 4% ABV, 15 IBUs.

American IPA: In the West Coast style, this IPA has plenty of malt backbone from pale and crystal malts, which support the big floral and citrus aromas from the American hop varieties used, plus a nice, smooth bitterness. 7.2% ABV, 52 IBUs.

HooDoo Stout: This dark brew straddles the line between an oatmeal and a sweet stout, as it is made with roasted barley, flaked oats, and lactose. Look for silkiness from the oats, a pleasing mouthfeel from the lactose, and coffee-like roastiness from the barley. It's something to sip on a winter's day in Fairbanks when it's -50 below outside! 5.8% ABV, 35 IBUs.

Extra Pale Ale: This brew uses Horizon and Santiam hops from Oregon to produce clear, smooth hop bitterness and a spicy hop aroma. The body is from American malt and has a clean, lightly toasted note to it. Bright and refreshing. 5.4% ABV, 49 IBUs.

Special and Seasonal Beers:

Bavarian Weissbier: The classic German summer beer, HooDoo's take on this style uses a true Bavarian yeast. This strain produces the banana, clove, and bubble gum notes which define this style. The beer is cloudy, crisp, effervescent, and refreshing, with a richness that comes from using German barley and wheat malts. 5% ABV, 10 IBUs.

Oktoberfest Lager: This beer pours a deep hazy orange color, with a tight, off white head. The aroma has rich malty notes from the 100% German malted barley used. Upon tasting, the beer is rich with malty sweetness and honey notes. A clean hop bitterness develops on the palate to balance it all out, then the beer finishes quite clean and dry, leaving a note of toasted bread. 5.6% ABV, 22 IBUs.

Distribution and Availability

HooDoo Brewing's beers are available almost exclusively at the brewery tap. HooDoo currently self-distributes to only five draft accounts in the Fairbanks area: the Golden Eagle Saloon (in Ester), the Fairbanks Curling Club, the University of Alaska–Fairbanks' Pub, the Turtle Club, and College Town Pizza. HooDoo has no plans to expand this distribution or begin packaging its beers.

Silver Gulch Brewing Company

Location: 2195 Old Steese Highway

Fox, Alaska 99712

Phone: (907) 452-2739

Email: matt@silvergulch.com

Website: www.silvergulch.com

Hours of Operation: Monday-Thursday 4pm-10pm. Friday 4pm-11pm. Saturday 11am-11pm. Sunday 11am-10pm.

Driving Directions: Leave Fairbanks travelling north on the Steese Highway. After approximately 10 miles, turn off onto the Old Steese Highway at the sign for Fox, AK. The brewery will be immediately on your right, across the highway from the Fox Roadhouse.

Overview

Originally opened in February, 1998, Silver Gulch Brewing and Bottling Company grew out of the homebrewing hobby of owner/founder Glenn Brady. Silver Gulch is the northernmost brewery or brewpub in the United States. While it took several years to achieve profitability, today Silver gulch has become one of the most successful breweries in Alaska, with its bottled beers being distributed statewide. In March 2007, Silver Gulch opened the restaurant and bar currently co-located with the brewery, and in 2008 an outdoor beer garden was added.

Many of its current recipes started out as Brady's homebrew recipes that were subsequently modified by long-time head brewer Levi Hansen. Hansen left Silver Gulch in the summer of 2013, and was succeeded as head brewer by Matt Austin.

Brewery Characteristics

Silver Gulch uses a 24-barrel brewhouse that was purchased from the Conner's Brewery in St. Catherines, Canada. Fermenters hold 75-barrels, and the 12,000 square foot brewery has a total fermentation capacity of 375 barrels.

Since Silver Gulch is located in such a remote area, it makes sense that it would be focused heavily on bottling its beers for sale around the state. After the beer has been conditioned at the brewery, it is cold-filtered through a state-of-the-art German system and then bottled on the 200 bottle-per-minute bottling system. This sterile filtration ensures shelf stability by removing the yeast from the beers.

Restaurant & Bar

Besides the brewery, the Silver Gulch complex in Fox also contains a bar and restaurant. The bar has a full liquor license (rather than operating under a brewery or brewpub license). Under Alaska law, this means the bar is allowed to serve hard alcohol, beers from other breweries, and is not limited in the amount per person per day. Silver Gulch takes advantage of this by offering an extensive selection of fine bottled beers from around the world, as well as a large selection of its on beers on draft.

Besides the bar, there is a well-appointed restaurant, open for dinner seven days a week and for lunch on the weekend. The food choices mix the standard pub fare of burgers and sandwiches with Alaskan favorites like salmon and halibut.

The bar at Silver Gulch. Note the glass-fronted beer cooler.

The Brewer Speaks

Head Brewer Matt Austin of Silver Gulch in his own words:

How did you become a commercial brewer?

"It was actually quite the serendipitous occasion. I arrived back to Alaska after a seven month road trip completely broke and jobless. With a huge interest in brewing but only experience as a home brewer and looking to get my foot in the door in the industry, I had been pestering Levi, the former head brewer here at Silver Gulch, for over a year to hire me to help out in the brewery. It just so happened that he was in need of some help at this exact time and was actually calling me to ask if I was interested. It was really great timing."

What do you see as the biggest challenges facing a craft brewer in Alaska?

"The distance and shipping challenges come to mind first. Mainly for properly managing and balancing your inventory of ingredients and supplies in order to never run out but also make sure you have enough storage when a huge shipment arrives. The distance and isolation also present a challenge in attempting to break into other markets with your product as well, especially concerning draft beer. Finally, the extreme seasonality also adds a bit of a challenge in planning, stocking up, and in keeping up inventory of your product. It is easy to get complacent when it is 40 below in January and February, but you need to keep your focus on the months ahead and preparing for the influx."

What characteristics do you think define Alaskan craft beer, as opposed to craft beer brewed elsewhere?

"Innovative, locally inspired, and unapologetic. Alaska is a unique and diverse state with a healthy arrogance and is extremely different from any other state. This tends to show in the beer that we produce up here. Yeah for the most part every brewery has their standard ambers and IPAs, but there are plenty of breweries pushing the envelope and using very uniquely Alaskan ingredients or at the very least putting their Alaskan spin on their brews. We have used rose hips, which are found everywhere up here, in our Wit, and we have also used locally and hand dug peat to smoke our own malt for our Scotch ale. These are just two examples of what we have done. There are many more from other breweries up here from using rhubarb or spruce tips, both very prevalent up here and fairly unique and bold additions to beer.

Where do you think Alaskan craft brewing in general and your brewery/brewpub in particular will be in eight to ten years?

"Alaskan craft brewing will continue the innovative, locally inspired, and unapologetic course that it is on right now. It will evolve with the brewing industry and continue to push the envelope while creating uniquely Alaskan beers and styles. There is plenty of room for growth up here so it would be great to see more breweries producing quality beers, adding to the already impressive craft beer culture up here, and hopefully making a great name for ourselves as Alaskan breweries in the lower 48 and throughout the world. It would be great to see our brewery continue to expand and further our reach into other markets and to start expanding our bottling and packaging to include our specialties and seasonals in order solidify our place as one of Alaska's top craft breweries."

The Beers

Regular Beers:

Coldfoot Pilsner Lager: This is a classic Bohemian-style pilsner, clean and crisp with the noble hop character such a style demands. 5.6% ABV, 30 IBUs. Available on draft and in 12 oz. bottles.

Pick Axe Porter: Hopped with Cascades. Very drinkable, with a deep brown-red color and a rich, malty flavor. An excellent session beer. 4.8% ABV, 25 IBUs. Available on draft and in 12 oz. bottles.

Fairbanks Lager: This is a Vienna-style lager. Munich malt gives it an amber color and a bit of malty sweetness, well-balanced with noble hops. 5.6% ABV, 18 IBUs. Available on draft and in 12 oz. bottles.

Copper Creek Amber Ale: An American Amber Ale hopped with Willamette hops, which give it a mild, pleasant and mildly spicy aroma. 4.8% ABV, 33 IBU's . Available on draft and in 12 oz. bottles.

Seasonal and Specialty Beers:

Epicenter Ale: An American Strong Ale brewed to commemorate the November 3, 2002 Denali Fault earthquake, 7.9 on the Richter scale and 7.9% ABV. Well-hopped with Willamettes to 40 IBUs.

Prudhoe Pig Oatmeal Rye Stout: The beer pours opaque with a nice tan head. The nose is sweet with some roasted oatmeal notes. On the palate there was some nice silkiness from the oats and some interesting spiciness on the finish from the rye. 5.7% ABV & 15 IBUs.

Osculum Infame Belgian Golden Winter Warmer: This beer is very crisp with interesting notes both from local spruce tips and 30 IBUs worth of noble Saaz hops. The grain bill includes both wheat and rye, along with enough barley to bring it in at 10.5% ABV, though you would not guess the brew was that potent when you taste it. A super beer to warm body and soul on those cold winter days in Fairbanks.

Distribution and Availability

Silver Gulch Brewing and Bottling Company's beers are widely available all across the state of Alaska. Of special note is their outlet on Concourse C at Anchorage International Airport. Since it is past the security checkpoint, travelers may purchase growlers to take as carry-on luggage during their flights home from Alaska, as well as sampling them at the bar.

Places to Find Craft Beer

Anchorage

Bars & Restaurants

Café Amsterdam

530 East Benson, Suite #3

907-274-0074   www.cafe-amsterdam.com/am/

Located in the same strip mall as La Bodega (see below), this is Anchorage's version of a Belgian "brown café". Look for a superb bottle selection, along with a rotating selection of excellent draft choices. Appropriate glassware is used.

Celestial Meads

600 W. 58th Ave.

907-250-8362   http://www.celestialmeads.com/

This is Anchorage's award-winning meadery. They are typically only open on Saturdays from 4 to 8 pm.

Eagle River Alehouse

11901 Old Glenn Highway, Eagle River

907-696-3000   http://er-alehouse.com/

Located in a northern suburb of Anchorage just off the Glenn Highway, this restaurant and alehouse has the largest tap selection in Alaska, with well over 50 beers on tap.

Firetap Alehouse & Restaurant

10950 O'Malley Centre Drive

(907) 561-2337   http://www.firetapalehouse.com

There are two Firetap locations in Anchorage, but for the real craft beer aficionado, there's only one, located in South Anchorage, near O'Malley Dr. On offer are 36 taps of local Alaska beers, plus an extensive bottled selection. Food is excellent, focusing on dishes prepared in their massive Fire Deck oven. There is also a good selection of wines and a full bar.

Humpy's Alaskan Alehouse

610 W. 6th Ave

907-276-2337   http://www.humpys.com/

The grand-daddy or beer bars in Anchorage, Humpy's (along with its next door siblings Sub-Zero Lounge and Flattop Pizza and Pool) remains one of the best places to find craft beer in town. A huge tap line, along with an extensive bottle selection.

McGinley's Pub

645 G St., Suite #101

907-279-1782   http://www.mcginleyspub.com/

Anchorage's version of an Irish pub. Look for a good food menu (nothing fried) and a decent beer selection.

Tap Root Public House

3300 Spenard Rd

907-345-0282   http://taprootalaska.com/

An eclectic pub with an unusual beer selection.

Package/Liquor Stores

La Bodega Wine Beer & Spirits

530 East Benson Blvd, Suite 5

907-569-3800   http://www.labodegastore.com/

Consistently voted the best beer store in Alaska. Sixteen tap growler bar. Extensive selection from many breweries in Alaska. Extremely knowledgeable staff.

Brown Jug Warehouse

4140 Old Seward Highway

907-563-3008   http://brownjugalaska.net/

This liquor store chain is quite ubiquitous in Anchorage and the Valley, but this is the location with the largest beer selection and a growler bar.

Festivals

Great Alaska Beer & Barley Wine Festival

Held each January in downtown Anchorage as the culmination of Alaska Beer Week, this festival has three sessions: Friday evening, Saturday afternoon, and Saturday evening. The Saturday afternoon session is known as the Connoisseurs' Session and features special beers. This is easily the biggest beer festival held in Alaska. http://auroraproductions.net/beer-barley.html

A small section of the Great Alaska Beer & Barley Wine Festival

The Culmination

Held in downtown Anchorage on a Saturday in late April or early May, this four-hour event is easily the most exclusive beer festival in Alaska. Organized by Gabe Fletcher of Anchorage Brewing Company, this event is limited to 300 attendees and sells out almost instantly. It features beers normally unavailable in Alaska. https://www.theculminationfestival.com

Bodega-Fest

Sponsored by La Bodega Wine Beer & Spirits, this festival is typically held on a Saturday in September at a park in Anchorage. http://labodegastore.com/events

Girdwood

Bars & Restaurants

Chair 5

171 Linblad Ave

(907) 783-2500   http://chairfive.com/

Smoke free. Serves lunch and dinner, 11 am to 1 am. Famous for deep dish square pizza, fresh ground gourmet burgers, and Alaskan seafood. Full bar, with over 60 craft brews, 30 single malts scotches, and 40 tequilas.

Wasilla/Palmer

Bars & Restaurants

Shwabenhof

Mile 6.5, Palmer-Wasilla Highway

907-357-2739

Billed as a German restaurant, this is actually a bar with a limited menu of pretzels, brats, and sauerkraut. However, it is in a beautiful location and has an excellent selection of both local and German beers.

Festivals

The Mighty Matanuska Brew Fest

This festival is held on a Friday and Saturday night in October at the State Fairgrounds in Palmer. There is shuttle bus service from Anchorage.
http://www.alaskastatefair.org/site/2013-mighty-matanuska-brewfest/

Talkeetna

Bars & Restaurants

The West Rib Pub & Grill

Main Street, (behind the general store)

907-733-3354   http://www.westribpub.info/

A popular local watering hole, this bar has a good selection of local Alaska beers and decently-priced burgers and pub grub.

Wildflower Café

Main St, (across from Denali Brewing/Twister Creek)

907-733-1782

http://www.talkeetnasuites.com/wildflower-cafe.html

If you can't get into Denali Brewing's beer garden or Twister Creek Restaurant across the road the 40 beers on tap here make it a good second choice.

Festivals

Talkeetna Beer Festival

Sponsored by Denali Brewing Company and The Denali Arts Council, this festival takes place on a Saturday in later September in downtown Talkeetna.
http://www.denaliartscouncil.org/events.htm

Denali Park/Healy

Bars & Restaurants

Prospector's Pizzeria & Alehouse

Mile 238.9 Parks Highway

907-683-7437   http://prospectorspizza.com/

Prospector's has over 50 beers on tap, with about have being from breweries across the state, including the nearby 49th State Brewing Company. There is also an extensive selection of well-chosen imports and bottled beers.

Festivals

Augtoberfest

49th State Brewing Company's answer to Oktoberfest, this two day event is held on the first weekend in August at the brewery. Live music and food vendors. http://49statebrewing.com

Ester

Bars & Restaurants

Golden Eagle Saloon

3630 Main St.

907-479-0809

An excellent bottles selection and several good brews on tap recommend this rustic saloon. This is a hangout for locals, and an excellent chance to escape the tourist bubble and rub shoulders with some real Alaskans.

Fairbanks

Bars & Restaurants

Lavelle's Bistro

575 First Ave

907-450-0555   http://www.lavellesbistro.com/

The place for some of the finest dining in Fairbanks, this restaurant has an excellent beer selection, though it chooses to emphasize its wine list.

The Pump House Restaurant

796 Chena Pump Rd.

907-479-8452   http://pumphouse.com/index.php

This restaurant has ten beers on tap, most of which are from local breweries, plus a decent bottled menu.

Package/Liquor Stores

Gold Hill

3040 Parks Highway

907-479-2333   http://www.goldhillalaska.com/

Located on the west side of the Parks Highway just south of Fairbanks proper, this small grocery and liquor store is famous for having the finest selection of bottled craft beers in Fairbanks.

Festivals

Golden Days Beer Fest

Sponsored by Silver Gulch Brewing and Bottling Company, this festival takes place on a Saturday in mid-July in the beer garden at their Fox, AK brewery. Besides the beers, there are food vendors and live music. www.silvergulch.com

Looking Ahead

The corridor from Anchorage to Fairbanks encompasses the heart of Alaska's craft brewing scene. Yes, there are many excellent craft breweries that lie outside of it, such as those on the Kenai Peninsula and Kodiak Island (covered in Volume I) and those in the panhandle of the state (to be covered in Volume III), but both the majority of Alaskans and Alaska's craft breweries fall within the region covered in this volume.

This area is by no means static. Many of the breweries in this region are feeling more than a bit pinched by the restrictions imposed by Alaska's fairly archaic and definitely confusing liquor laws. Efforts are underway to revise these laws and ease the restrictions on breweries and brewpubs as far as how much beer they can produce and sell through various outlets. If these efforts are successful, it would certainly encourage further expansion by several of the breweries covered in this volume.

Besides plans for possible expansion by the existing breweries, there are several other breweries in the planning stages. The date for a new brewery to open is always a moving target, subject to the vagaries of bank financing and government licensing, but a couple of new breweries are definitely in the advanced planning stages. Keep your eye out for the likes of Chugach Brewing Company under owner/brewer Brandon Hall and North Star Brewing under owner and former Broken Tooth Head Brewer Clarke Pelz. There are continual rumors of a brewery or brewpub in Girdwood, though to date there are no names attached to the project.

Finally, in many ways this area of the state has the most mature craft beer palate in Alaska. Over the past few years the number of festivals and food-beer pairing events held in this part of the state has skyrocketed. I fully expect that their numbers will continue to increase for the foreseeable future.

Speaking of the future, look for the third volume of ***Beer on the Last Frontier: Southeast Alaska Breweries*** to be released in 2014, along with an up-dated version combining all three volumes in a single work.

Until Next Time, Cheers!

About the Authors

One of the first questions I always ask about any guidebook is this: "What qualifies the author to give me advice on this particular subject or place?" So I think it's only fair that I answer that question by telling you a little bit about myself.

I've been a craft beer lover and homebrewer since 1989. From 1984 to 2004, I was an officer in the United States Navy, which allowed me to travel extensively and sample beers all over the world. From 1998 to 2001, I was fortunate enough to be stationed in London, and during those three years I travelled throughout Britain, as well as to Belgium, Germany, and the Czech Republic to sample the best beers each had to offer.

I retired from the Navy in 2004 and moved to Sterling on Alaska's Kenai Peninsula, taking a job at Kenai Peninsula College, which is part of the University of Alaska. As craft breweries and brewpubs began opening in the area, I convinced my college administration that it was time to offer a course on beer, and in the spring of 2007, I taught *The Art & History of Brewing* for the first time. It was a rousing success and I have taught it again each year since.

Given the popularity of my course, starting a blog seemed the next logical step. My purpose in writing Drinking on the Last Frontier was mainly to keep my students, current and former, apprised of local beer developments. Much to my surprise, my blog developed quite a following, both within and outside of Alaska. Its popularity was such that I was offered a monthly beer column in one of our local papers, **The Redoubt Reporter**, in November 2009.

2/27/2010 at the Wynkoop Brewing Company in Denver

As I was riding the wave of this success, my wife convinced me to enter the **Wynkoop Brewing Company**'s Beerdrinker of the Year contest in December 2009. I didn't think I had much of a chance, but I was selected as one of the three finalists, and in the head-to-head competition in Denver on February 27, 2010, I actually won, much to my amazement. Deciding to accept this as a sign, my wife and I attended the Great American Beer Festival that year, something I hadn't done since 1990.

Since then, I have continued my efforts to educate folks about craft beer and to promote Alaska's craft breweries, both within and outside the 49th state. In 2012, I was hired by the **Northwest Brewing News** as their correspondent for Alaska, and I also began working on this book project.

You will certainly notice the many excellent photographs which illustrate this book. These are the work of my beautiful and talented wife, Elaine Howell, who graciously agreed to take part in this project by supplying those photographs.

The authors, Elaine and Bill Howell

This book is the second in a series of three volumes which describe the state of play of craft brewing in Alaska. As with any such guidebook, you may find that things have changed at a particular brewery since the time of writing; if so, please accept my apologies in advance. I intend to do my best to update this work on a regular basis, but the craft brewing scene in this state is a fast-moving target.

In spite of any such shortcomings, I hope you will find this work enlightening, entertaining, and useful. It represents a small gift back on my part to all the brewers who work hard every day to give us such exceptional beers to enjoy and to the citizens of the magnificent state of Alaska, which is now my home.